From:

_____

_____

To:

_____

_____

_____

Against All Odds

Overcoming Challenges and
Achieving Success in Life

SEUN AKINLOTAN

AGAINST ALL ODDS
Overcoming Challenges and Achieving Success in Life

© 2023 by Seun Akinlotan

No portion of this book may be reproduced, stored in a retrieval system, or transmitted in any form or by any means–electronic, mechanical, photocopy, recording, scanning, or other–except for brief quotations in critical articles or reviews without the prior written permission of the publisher or author.

Although every precaution has been taken to verify the accuracy of the information contained herein, the author and publisher assume no responsibility for any errors or omissions. No liability is accepted for damages resulting from using the information contained within.

Unless otherwise stated, all scripture quotations are from the New International Version of the Bible.

You may purchase a copy of this purchased by contacting the Author and Publisher at:

hello@seunakinlotan.com

info@hadarcreations.com

Cover Outfit: Olubukola Olawale

Cover Photograph: Atinuke Dami-Yakubu

Cover and Interior Design: Seyi Daniels

Published by: Hadar Creations

ISBN: 978-0-9995833-2-6 (Hardcover)

ISBN: 978-0-9995833-3-3 (Paperback)

Printed in the United States of America

Contents

Dedication	iv
Acknowledgement	v
Advance Praise for Against All Odds	vii
Introduction	ix
1 In the Beginning	1
2 Making a Mountain out of Almost Nothing	19
3 Gaining Clarity	33
4 Catapulting into the Limelight	47
5 Stooping to Conquer	61
6 Overcoming Roadblocks	75
7 Stirring the Stagnant Waters	89
8 Understanding Cultures	115
9 From Setbacks to Stepping Up	127
10 Soaring Through Limitations	137
Conclusion	151
Bibliography	155

Dedication

In the eternal remembrance of a remarkable woman, my beloved mother, Grace Bolanle Ogunjobi, whose extraordinary existence, triumphant endeavors, and notable accomplishments have ignited a blazing passion within me to transcend the confines of ordinary living, this book stands as an unwavering dedication to her indomitable spirit. With heartfelt gratitude, I salute you, Mom, for gracing this world with your awe-inspiring existence. Your everlasting and profound legacy shall be cherished and safeguarded for future generations.

Acknowledgments

The creation of this book stands as a testament to the grace of God and the unwavering support of the remarkable people He has blessed me with. I am deeply grateful for the divine assistance that guided me through the challenges I encountered during the writing process and for the grace that enabled me to overcome seemingly insurmountable obstacles and publish this book.

My heartfelt appreciation goes to the love of my life, strong pillar, and darling husband, Oluseyi, whose sacrifices for me and our children are mindblowing.

I am indebted to my children, whose steadfast support was a constant source of motivation, even when I contemplated giving up. Their encouragement and unwavering belief in me propelled me forward, allowing me to persevere and complete this project.

I'd also like to express my profound gratitude to:

My siblings, Oluwafolakemi, Oluwadaisi, and Omotola with whom we created childhood unforgettable memories together.

My dear and influential Pastor, Funmi Obilana whose words of wisdom daily permeate my soul, bringing out the best in me.

My blessed and purposeful friends, Dr. Oluwaseun Ogunjimi who went above and beyond to contribute her story, be my sounding board and offer words of encouragement, and Pastor Temitope Ibrahim who painstakingly reviewed an advance copy of this book despite her hectic schedule.

My SA core team, Okikiola Olusanu, Dr. Omotola Ajayi, Tolulope Oluwole, Omolola Apoeso, and Oluwakemi Eko whose sacrifices, day in and day out afforded me the energy I needed to keep going.

My delectable, godly, and sweet sister, and mentee, Oluwatosin Arodudu, for her unwavering support, prayers and standing by me from the beginning of this project to the end.

I am also indebted to my publisher, Hadar Creations, whose patience, doggedness and hard work made this project a reality. They went above and beyond their responsibilities to ensure this book is a masterpiece.

Furthermore, I am deeply grateful to my graphic design team, extended family, friends, inner circle, accountability partners, and well-wishers. Their consistent inquiries about the progress of this book and solid support provided the motivation and encouragement I needed to keep going.

Thank you so much for standing by my side and supporting me throughout this journey against all odds.

Advance Praise for Against All Odds

"Seun's book is a true masterpiece! She wrote it during a time in her life when the odds were stacked against her, yet she persevered and created this book. This achievement speaks volumes about pushing past the challenges life presents us with. In it, you will find real-life stories of courage, determination, and resilience in adversity. It is a testament that we can all overcome the odds and achieve our wildest dreams. The relatable stories and principles presented in the book make it easy to understand and implement in our own lives. Reading it instills hope and confidence and equips us with the tools to bridge the gap to succeed despite the obstacles. Seun writes passionately, providing actionable steps anyone serious about success can take to achieve it against all odds. This book is a must-read for those determined to succeed!"

Temitope Ibrahim
Author, The Secrets to Your Win.

"As we journey through life, obstacles often appear along the way, almost taunting us with the phrase, "You signed up for us!" But how do we succeed despite these challenges? Seun Akinlotan's book, AGAINST ALL ODDS, offers practical solutions to this question. A woman with a spirit of excellence, Seun has created a masterpiece that gives readers the tools to overcome any obstacle life throws their way. Seun's ability to transform adversity into opportunity is awe-inspiring. Even when thrust into a leadership role at a young age, she refused to let life's challenges shape her personality or hold her back from achieving her goals. Instead, she used each obstacle as a stepping stone for personal growth, which has made her the phenomenal woman she is today. In addition, she has committed herself to helping others overcome their obstacles and become their best selves, no matter their challenges. Seun poured her heart and soul into AGAINST ALL ODDS, and her passion for helping others shines through in the relatable and unique ideas presented within its pages.

The language used in the book is simple and easy to understand, making it accessible to readers of all levels of expertise. Furthermore, the call to action points provided at the end of each chapter are practical and applicable, enabling readers to put what they have learned into practice. I frequently referred to these steps, which made a significant difference in implementing the principles shared in the book. I highly recommend AGAINST ALL ODDS to anyone seeking to conquer obstacles and succeed. It's an inspiring read that will leave you feeling motivated and empowered to take on the world, no matter the challenges that lie ahead. Seun's insights are invaluable, and her commitment to helping others is commendable. This book is a must-read for anyone looking to overcome adversity and reach their full potential."

Oluwatosin O. Arodudu,
Publisher and Identity Coach, Hadar Creations.

Introduction

Growing up as a girl in a society that saw women as second-class citizens was tough. But witnessing my mother's struggles within the walls of our home fueled my determination to rise above the patriarchy.

Despite being born into a family of seven girls and facing numerous obstacles to education and career advancement, Grace, my mother, refused to be held back. Her unwavering determination to spread her wings and fly was awe-inspiring. Not only did she embrace her status as a mother of only daughters, but she also instilled strong values that have shaped us into who we are today.

An irresistible force, a master at turning brilliant ideas into profitable businesses in no time and a fierce opponent of self-pity, Grace believed in the dignity of labor. Her unwavering work ethic and enterprising spirit left an indelible mark on me.

She witnessed the beginning of this book, and I even shared copies of the first draft and the preliminary design of the cover page with her.

However, before finishing the writing of this work, she unexpectedly and suddenly transitioned to glory. Her demise was a cruel blow and the most bitter pill I have had to swallow. Her untimely death and the cascading events that unfolded drove me to the point of deep confusion, disappointment, and hurt such that I felt my whole life was crumbling beneath my feet.

Amidst the chaos of deep confusion, disappointment, and hurt, I was on the verge of throwing in the towel. The weight was crushing, and I felt like drowning in despair. But then, just when I thought I couldn't go on, I was reminded of all the times I had overcome adversity. Through the darkest moments of my life, God has been my constant guide, always there for me unconditionally. With renewed strength, I persevered, pushing through to finally publish "AGAINST

ALL ODDS." I can almost see Grace looking down on me from heaven, smiling with pride and joy.

As you hold this book, chances are you are looking for a way to break free from feeling stuck and hopeless. Let me tell you, I've been there. I know what it's like to feel like you've hit a wall and have no idea how to move forward. I remember praying for longer nights to have more time to brainstorm solutions. And if that wasn't enough, I had a job offer rescinded just weeks after I thought I had it in the bag. But I didn't allow those setbacks to defeat me. Instead, I found a way to keep moving forward, and now I'm here to share some proven strategies with you.

Are you tired of feeling defeated by life's challenges? It's time to change the narrative. Instead of seeing obstacles as monsters trying to hold you back, what if you saw them as opportunities to propel yourself forward? That's the mindset I want to share in my book, AGAINST ALL ODDS. Let's conquer our circumstances together and achieve success, no matter what life throws our way.

Against All Odds is the book for you if you want to unlock your true potential and achieve lasting success against all odds. In it, I share stories of everyday people like you and me who overcame incredible challenges to become game-changers, pacesetters, and trailblazers. Whether facing hurdles at work, in your personal life, or just feeling stuck, I'm confident that the powerful lessons and inspiring examples I've included will help you unleash your full potential and achieve your wildest dreams.

This book is not just another self-help guide; it's an invaluable treasure trove of principles that will help you unlock endless possibilities. With captivating true-life stories, insightful advice, and practical strategies, it's the ultimate guide to achieving success. If you've been searching for a guide to inspire, motivate, and challenge you to be your best, look no further than this book.

You hold in your hands a true masterpiece. As you turn its pages, get ready for a life-changing journey. I have carefully crafted each word to guide you toward a life of independence and fulfillment. Also, you will discover simple and actionable nuggets that will lead you toward a life of abundance and purpose. This book is a testament to the fact that God created you for greatness, and it is time to embrace the will of God for your life. So why wait? Start your journey to greatness today!

Debunking the Myths

This book is your key to unlocking a world of possibilities you may not have thought possible. Prepare to challenge the traditional notions of success that have been holding you back for far too long. You'll discover how to debunk the myths about success passed down through generations based on gender, socioeconomic status, educational background, and geographic location. With this knowledge, you can break free from limitations and explore the abundance of opportunities available.

Where Success Thrives

Are you ready to break free from the constraints that have held you back from achieving your dreams and aspirations? This book will revolutionize your mindset about success. Success thrives in an environment where people are open-minded. It's time to abandon the old myths and theories passed down for generations and embrace the proven principles that have consistently yielded results. Success is not reserved for a select few; it's available to anyone who desires it and is willing to do the work. With this book, you'll gain the tools and knowledge to seize the opportunities around you and never settle for less than what you truly deserve.

Getting the Most Out of This Book

My primary objective is to impart valuable insights from my vast experiences and others so that you can overcome life's challenges and ultimately achieve your aspirations. Consider the following steps to get the most value out of this book:

◊ Have a notepad and pen handy: Jot down any insightful ideas or revelations from reading this book.

◊ Read alone: Start by reading the book in solitude, absorbing the content, internalizing it, and taking relevant actions.

◊ Read with others: Consider forming a mastermind or study group to read this book together. Doing so will expand your insights and enrich your perspective on life.

◊ Apply the principles: Knowledge is only valid when applied. Actively search for opportunities to apply the principles in your daily life.

◊ Track your progress: To notice improvement over time, establish systems to track and measure your progress as you learn how to succeed.

- CHAPTER ONE -

In the Beginning

"Life is progress and not a station."
Ralph Waldo Emerson

More than forty years ago, an adventurous young couple from the bustling city of Lagos, Nigeria, boldly decided to embark on a quest for a better life. Leaving behind the familiar comforts of their hometown, they set their sights on the scenic enclave of Abeokuta, popularly known as the "Rock City," in Ogun State, Nigeria.

Drawn by the city's proximity to Lagos, its renowned education system, and the nurturing environment it provided for raising children, the couple saw Abeokuta as a land of endless possibilities. A melting pot of cultural diversity, it offered a promising future and a chance to partake in a thriving industry and an economy ripe for growth. And so, with steely determination and unbridled optimism, they embarked on a journey that would change their lives forever.

As fate would have it, just before embarking on a life-changing trip, the couple was blessed with a precious gift - a baby girl. But it was no ordinary pregnancy. The road to delivery was arduous, and the couple had to summon enormous strength to make it through. Thankfully, their prayers were answered, and God rewarded them with a beautiful and healthy baby. In a testament of gratitude, they named her Oluwaseun, meaning "Thank you, God."

The new parents, eager to start a new life, left the bustling city of Lagos for the serene suburbs of Abeokuta, popularly known as "Rock City." The transition was not without its challenges, especially for the new mother.

Grace, my mother, grew up in Lagos. Relocating to the suburbs of Rock City, away from what she had known all her life was tough. She left behind her family, her social network, a thriving enterprise, and all the help she could have enjoyed from her siblings in raising her children. In addition, Rock City provided different opportunities for her to thrive than Lagos. It was not an easy transition, mainly because there was no technology to connect with loved ones, and she started her life afresh. But with grit and determination, she found a way to adapt and flourish.

Fast forward to the present day, and that resilient and beautiful baby girl has grown into a strong and accomplished woman, Seun Akinlotan - the author of "Against All Odds," the book you are presently reading.

Life in Rock City was a wild ride, a beautiful blend of highs and lows, twists and turns, and everything in between. As a young girl, I called one of the most stunning neighborhoods in town my home, surrounded by towering structures that took my breath away.

Despite the awe-inspiring scenery, what I loved most about my neighborhood was its serene ambiance, perfect for families like mine. On weekdays, my sisters and I headed off to school, taking a leisurely walk with our neighborhood pals, cherishing each step and enjoying every moment of our journey.

After a long day of learning, I attended private tutorial sessions organized by a few of my teachers, where I sharpened my cognitive skills and soaked up new knowledge. And when Saturday rolled around, it was time for household chores - washing clothes, folding laundry, and cleaning the floors and yard. It was a time of bonding and hard work, a perfect balance of responsibility and play.

Grace was a woman of great initiative who despised idleness, and as such, she taught my siblings and me the value of hard work. Through her guidance, I learned how to use a hand hoe to create mounds for planting tuber crops like yams and cassava. We also maintained a small garden, cultivating various vegetables, fruits, and legumes that provided fresh produce for our daily meals.

Moreover, my mother taught me how to care for my younger siblings and be a role model to them. She frequently held me accountable for their wrongdoings. While I grasped the essence of most of her teachings, it was challenging for me to understand why that was so.

Since the age of six (6), I have noticed Grace's deep passion for education. She instilled in me the belief that an educated girl would grow up to be an unstoppable woman, leaving an impact that would transcend generations. Inspired by her words, I dreamed of fulfilling my purpose while helping others achieve theirs. After dinner, my mother would share fables and folktales with my siblings and me in the evenings. She would cleverly weave lessons and values from our daily experiences, leaving a lasting impression on us.

After winding down for the night, she would gather us for prayers, during which I learned many of the Psalms I effortlessly recite by heart to this day. Psalm 91, which speaks about total trust in God as our protector, was and is still my favorite. She was also stubborn about signing us up for activities that would stimulate our spiritual growth. One such move was joining the Emmanuel Bible Club, where elementary school children met weekly to learn more about Jesus and what it meant to be a faithful born-again Christian. I enjoyed attending this club far more than Sunday school at our local church.

Our teachers, to whom my heart sends blessings, generously volunteered their time to ensure we were firmly grounded in our faith. I even had the opportunity to represent the club at various annual competitions. My favorite activity was the "memory verse," which tested a child's ability to recall a particular text from the Bible that they had memorized. It was a mental challenge that I thoroughly enjoyed.

Around the time I was seven years old, I remember a day when I went to town with my father, Ade. I sat in the back seat, thrilled to have some alone time with him as we headed to our preferred grocery store to buy butter. As children, our favorite go-to meal was bread and butter; this store was the only one that seemed to stock our famous butter brand. Or it was simply my father's preferred store.

We passed a man standing in front of a store as we drove home. My dad recognized him as Segun (not his real name), an acquaintance, but we had already gone a few miles ahead. Ade hit the brakes without hesitation and backed up to talk to him. After exchanging pleasantries for a few minutes, Segun noticed I was in the car. "Is this your child?" he asked with curiosity.

My dad confirmed that I was indeed his child and shared how God had blessed him with three beautiful daughters. I could immediately see the expression on Mr. Segun's face change from excitement to bewilderment.

"You mean you have three girls?!" he exclaimed.

Once again, my dad confirmed it to be accurate, and Segun's countenance dropped as if he had just received the worst news of his life, filled with pity for my father.

After the encounter, I asked my dad why the man had seemed so downcast upon discovering he was raising three girls.

"Don't mind him," he answered curtly.

Although I obeyed and didn't press him further, I couldn't help but wonder why Segun's reaction had been so hostile toward having three daughters. The question lingered in my mind.

Several months had passed since the encounter with Mr. Segun when my mom and I went to the open-air market to do some shopping. As with most markets in Nigeria, bargaining was necessary for making good purchases, making me dread going there with my mom. Spending an entire day moving from stall to stall in search of the best bargains was tiring, and by the time we returned home, I often found it hard to justify the efforts with the purchased items.

At the market that day, I overheard a butcher tell my mom that having only daughters was terrible. According to him, a girl would end up in a man's kitchen and render any investment in her education useless. His words deeply affected me, and to this day, I still remember them vividly. I have a sharp memory and tend to remember details that catch my attention, even from a young age. For instance, I still recall the dresses I wore to parties when I was three. So, the butcher's statement left a lasting impression on me.

Unbeknownst to Grace, I held onto those words and similar comments by some of our extended family members and silently pondered on them. As I grew older, I became more aware of the societal pressure on women to bear male children. Rather than serve as a source of discouragement, my awareness of societal pressure on women only fueled my determination to succeed, as a female, against all odds.

A New Life

It was barely past midnight when a ray of light caught my attention from across the hallway. I wondered why it appeared there so early, as I just wanted to sleep. I cp like a snail into its shell, turned my back, and pulled the covers over my head. I dozed off for a minute but woke up soon due to movements around the house. Despite this, I stayed in bed as I needed to rest before my morning routine would start by 5 a.m.

And then, boom! The unexpected occurred suddenly: Grace entered my room to wake me up. She clutched her protruded belly and told me, in barely audible sounds, her face contorted with so much pain that she was about to have the baby. I knew the baby was due and got the "message." I was like my mom's assistant and was involved in every phase of the pregnancy, so I understood every of her spoken and unspoken words.

Although I was disappointed that my sleep was interrupted, I was also joyous that the baby boy I had been praying for might finally be arriving.

Groggily, I stumbled out of bed to help her pack the contents of the hospital bag. In Nigeria, it is common for women in labor to bring their supplies to the hospital. While preparing the bag, my mom informed me we would have to walk to the hospital.

"Walk?" I exclaimed in disbelief.
"Yes, we will walk to the
hospital," she confirmed.

The news that we had to trek to the hospital filled me with dread and anxiety. I was overwhelmed with "what ifs?"

and could not hold back my tears. I silently prayed for three things as we stepped out with the bag resting on my head:

◊ We would encounter a Good Samaritan on our way.

◊ That my mother would arrive safely at the hospital.

◊ That the newborn would be a boy.

Outside was pitch-black and eerily quiet, as if the world held its breath. I was unsure if we had the strength to make it to the hospital on time, and the thought of my mother giving birth on the roadside terrified me.

As we trudged along, I heard a distant sound of an approaching vehicle. My heart leaped with hope as the headlights drew nearer, and I prayed that the driver would stop to help us. To my utter dismay, the driver drove past us. My heart immediately shattered because my mom could barely walk at that point on the journey, increasing the likelihood that she would deliver the baby by the roadside.

However, the car eventually slowed down, and the driver backed up toward us with the window rolled down.

> "Are you in need of help?" the driver asked concernedly.

I explained our situation, and he offered to ride us to the hospital without hesitation. My heart filled with gratitude as we finally climbed into the car, relieved to find a good Samaritan. We later learned that he worked at a local news station and was on his way to dispatch some deliverables at a distribution center. Reflecting on that experience now, I am grateful for the kindness of strangers and the power of prayer. It taught me that even in the darkest moments, hope and help are available and that one should never give up.

Upon our arrival at the hospital, only one nurse was in the building. She was half awake, leading me to harbor misgivings about her competence in assisting my mom with the delivery process, especially since there were no doctors or other medical professionals On-site. The nurse also seemed uneasy when she realized Grace was in labor and set to deliver the baby. I recall her asking pertinent questions during the admission process, but my mom kept repeating, "The baby is here."

Shortly after, the situation escalated into an emergency, causing the nurse to start pacing anxiously in the hallway. I tried to follow closely behind but could not access the room. Within moments, she retrieved a stretcher, helped my mother lie on it, and swiftly transported her into the delivery room without saying a word to me.

Nonetheless, the exit area was outfitted with sizable transparent glass louvers, allowing me to observe the childbirth process unfolding. Standing outside, I wept and prayed fervently, overcome with dread at the mere thought of losing my mother.

Thankfully, the birthing process went smoothly, and my mother gave birth to the baby within just 15 minutes - an unforgettable experience permanently etched in my memory.

As I awaited the nurse's announcement of the baby's gender, I couldn't help but wonder what my reaction would be if the baby turned out to be another girl. I had fervently prayed that my mother would give birth to a male child, hoping to spare her from the constant harassment and painful humiliation she faced from people. When the nurse emerged from the delivery room and began to make her way toward the exit, I hurriedly asked her about the baby's gender.

"It is a girl!" she exclaimed joyfully.

Struggling to comprehend the news, I slumped against the wall, landed on my backside, and began to weep uncontrollably as if something terrible had befallen us. Despite God blessing my family with a new life, I couldn't help feeling unhappy, knowing the weight of the burden ahead for my mother after the delivery.

When the nurse finally allowed me access to the delivery room, my mom took a look at me and reminded me that "a new life is a blessing and not a curse." While I fully agreed with her positive outlook, in my thoughts, I was consumed by the reality of living in a patriarchal society where having male children was deemed more valuable than having female ones.

Nevertheless, my mom's words provided the comforting reassurance I needed to cope with the sobering reality we were facing.

Upon returning home, the news of my mom giving birth to another girl elicited mixed reactions from our family and friends. Nevertheless, Grace remained unwavering in her upbeat and indomitable spirit. She knew that the gender of the child was beyond her control and instead focused on the things she could influence.

> "Results will cancel insults," she would often remark as she emphasized the importance of focusing on our actions rather than the opinions of others.

She channeled all her energy into bringing up her daughters in the best way possible rather than sulking over circumstances beyond her control. Her actions led me to often marvel at her ability to remain poised and calm, even amid the most turbulent storms.

The Power of Understanding Your Identity

Grace was a resilient woman who maintained her unique identity. Even during tumultuous times, she remained steadfast in her faith and refused to be swayed by societal expectations or current events that did not align with her values. She would often advise me to "stand tall everywhere you go."

Whenever I returned from school and shared my experiences with her, she would remind me that "you are more than a conqueror in Christ Jesus." From a young age, she instilled an unwavering belief that God had fearfully and wonderfully made me and that I could achieve anything I set my mind to, regardless of the obstacles ahead.

Grace placed great importance on how her daughters dressed and was always willing to invest her time, energy, and resources to ensure that we were appropriately attired and looked our best. From childhood until we could shop for ourselves, Grace would make regular trips to Lagos to buy clothes.

As I experimented with high-heeled shoes, my mom would share stories of how she wore them confidently as a teenager. "Your confidence shines through in how you walk," Grace told me. If she noticed me slouching or not walking correctly, she would remind me to stand up straight, a habit I still maintain today.

During my formative years, I used to think my mom was too meticulous about things, but I later understood that paying attention to detail can boost confidence. She had established her identity in Christ and instilled this value in her children's lives, which paid off tremendously.

Now, each time I face challenges, I picture how she would have handled such a situation if she were in my shoes while I also align my responses and actions with God's words.

One of my favorite Bible verses, 1 Peter 2:9, reads, "But you are a chosen people, a royal priesthood, a holy nation, God's special possession, that you may declare the praises of him who called you out of darkness into his wonderful light." This verse reassures me of my royal identity, making me feel confident that God is mindful of me and that I can overcome any obstacle or challenge.

Do you know who you are? Are you clear about your unique identity? Knowing and affirming your identity can provide security and confidence, especially during challenging times. It can help you stay focused on your goals and resiliently navigate obstacles. Understanding who you are and your purpose can also provide a sense of direction and help you make essential decisions in life.

You Are Valuable

As an environmental scientist, I have visited numerous industries to learn about their waste management practices. One such sector is a gold refining facility I had the opportunity to visit several years ago. The facility refines raw gold before being sent to customers. When my boss informed me of the need to visit this facility, I saw it as a once-in-a-lifetime chance to witness the transformation of gold firsthand. It was a rare and valuable opportunity to deepen my understanding, as I had only read about its refining process before.

On the day of the scheduled visit, I arrived at the facility with a smile, eager to learn. However, upon seeing the building, I was taken aback by its unassuming appearance. I even wondered if I had come to the right place, checking my map repeatedly until I confirmed that I had arrived at the intended location.

As I approached the entrance, a representative greeted me and showed me around. He was a tall, plump man in his early sixties and introduced himself as John (not his real name) with a warm smile.

"Welcome to our facility," he announced.

"It's my pleasure to have you here today."

I introduced myself, and we exchanged pleasantries before he offered me a brief overview of what I could expect during the tour.

Our first stop was the research and development laboratory, where various tests were conducted. I was curious to see a sample of unrefined gold, so I asked if it was allowed.

The selection was in powder form and looked like dirt. If I had encountered it anywhere outside of the laboratory, I would have thought it was just regular dirt.

"You seem to have a good grasp of how things work around here," I quipped, impressed by his extensive knowledge of the refining process.

"I've been working here for over 30 years, so it's become second nature to me," he replied warmly.

The experience kept playing in my mind as I headed home that day. I could not help but be intrigued at how unrefined gold, which could easily be mistaken for a worthless object, is incredibly valuable. Its intrinsic worth remains the same, regardless of whether anyone recognizes its value.

Like gold, you are intrinsically valuable, regardless of any external factors such as gender, location, ethnicity, socio-economic or educational background, religious beliefs, or any other classification. And just like gold, your value remains unchanged even if others fail to recognize or acknowledge it.

However, your value can only increase over time if you commit to undergoing a refining process. The value of refined gold is always higher than raw gold.

Similarly, investing in self-improvement and personal growth can increase your weight over time, much like how compound interest accumulates.

Are you interested in shining brighter and increasing your value? Then commit to a refining process. This process is advantageous. It may involve learning new things, unlearning old habits or beliefs, and sometimes relearning stuff you thought you already knew.

So, if you're ready to embark on this journey and become more valuable, now is the time to take action to refine your life. It requires determination and a willingness to make changes along the way. It involves stretching yourself out of your comfort zone and embracing new challenges. And when you diligently follow through, you will become the best version of yourself and reach your full potential.

Stand Guard over the Door of Your Heart

One thing I have learned to do for a long while is to stand guard over the door of my heart. It entails being mindful of what I allow into my heart and mind because it can shape my beliefs, thoughts, and actions. Everyone who wants to surmount life's difficulties and achieve success should also commit to mastering this.

Handling the door of your heart is an essential skill you need to succeed against all odds. What you allow into it and feed it with can significantly impact your life. As a Christian, I understand that my heart is the seat of power, and whatever I feed it with can significantly impact your life. As a Christian, I understand that my heart is the seat of power, and whatever I feed into it shapes my belief system, controls my thoughts, and ultimately determines how I react to or handle the curveballs life throws at me.

When you guard your heart, you are also protecting your emotional well-being. It helps you to avoid the negative influence of toxic people, situations, and circumstances that can drain your energy and enthusiasm. Doing this lets you stay focused on your goals and take actions that align with your aspirations.

Standing guard over the door of your heart is a powerful tool for personal growth, development, and success. It enables you to take control of your life and steer it in the desired direction rather than being tossed around by external forces.

I recall a touching tale about a hard-of-hearing businessman who managed a roadside business selling fresh akara1 (bean cakes) with the help of his son. As time passed, his son got college admission, becoming the first in their family to attend a tertiary institution. Attaining this milestone was an emotional moment for the father, who cherished his son deeply.

As his son prepared to leave, he presented his father with a radio set, a prized possession when television sets were non-existent. While the son was away at college, a severe recession hit the city, causing hardship for many.

The city's financial experts provided daily updates about the volatile situation on the radio, often presenting a bleak outlook. The economic crisis led to widespread panic and decreased spending, causing many businesses to shut down.

Despite the circumstances, the businessman remained unaware of the distressing news because he had difficulty hearing, leaving him unaffected by the experts' predictions of doom. He remained committed to his business, showing up daily enthusiastically. He dedicated himself to enhancing his recipe, providing exceptional customer service, and honing his skills in preparing flavorful akara, which resulted in an expanded customer base.

His devoted patrons became evangelists for his delicious bean cakes, spreading the word about their delectable taste across the region. As a result, he experienced a surge in sales, profits, and overall business growth, even amidst a recession.

When his son returned from college one day, he was surprised by his father's exploits despite the recession.

> "Dad, did you hear about the recession that hit our region?" he asked curiously.

> "No, my focus has been on growing our business," his father replied with a warm smile on his wrinkle-stricken face.

The son explained the recession and the importance of scaling back to his dad. As soon as his father understood the projections of the existing trends, he felt the pressing need to comply and started cutting back on his business operations. What happened after that? The collapse of a thriving business during a recession.

Embedded in this story are lessons on the fundamental necessity of standing guard over the door of one's heart. The father allowed his son's information to lead him to an alternate reality.

As human beings, we are moved mainly by what we see, hear, or read. The onus is on us to constantly filter every piece of information and separate the potentially harmful and beneficial ones. The results we get or do not get are the ultimate products of our thoughts.

Are you wondering how to stand guard over the door of your heart? Start by being intentional about what you read, watch, and listen to. There are television shows designed to control how and what you think in a manner that is detrimental to your well-being. This harmful content is often subtly infused into the media you consume, but if you're mindful enough to scrutinize what you watch, you will discern and carefully sift through it. If you desire to overcome challenges and achieve success in life, you must be the strictest censor of the content you consume from time to time as you proceed.

Social media is another platform that can be a conduit for negative messages to one's heart. In the early days of networking sites, they seemed the perfect place to meet people. I remember the first time I reconnected with a few high school and college friends with whom I had already lost contact. It felt surreal. Connecting with people at the click of a button was an out-of-the-world experience for me, but as more people began to join my list, coupled with the tendency to reach others outside of my immediate circle, things began to spiral.

Suppose you are unintentional about the types of people you interact with. If you read or swallow every opinion shared on social media hook, line, and sinker, you might be allowing harmful content to seep into your heart, one word per time.

Standing guard over the door of your heart is vital because the information that flows into your heart controls your thoughts, and your thoughts direct your actions — in that order. As someone who dreams of becoming great in life, even with the odds stacked against you, you must be careful about the information you allow to take root in your subconscious.

Another way you can stand guard over the door of your heart is to be picky about the kinds of people you spend time with. A school of thought posits that each man is an average of the five people he spends the most time with, and I could not agree more. In truth, the people you spend significant time with influence your choices and decisions. If you keep tinkering away your precious time with those who effortlessly see and magnify insurmountable obstacles in opportunities, sooner or later, you will be mentally conditioned and re-wired to run away from golden opportunities disguised as challenges.

I appreciate the Yoruba language and learned a lot while growing up. In the Yoruba language, an adage corroborates this line of thought, and I can loosely translate it thus: "A sheep that becomes a dog's close companion is certain to feed on poop."

We are social beings and wired to do what our friends do. Think about your current closest friends. What decisions have they made over time? How have your friends' decisions affected yours? Do you notice any patterns? If you are reasonably objective in your responses to these three questions, you will realize that the company you keep influences you.

If you associate with friends who capitulate in the face of the slightest obstruction, more likely than not, you will do the same. Remember that having friends whose words light up a fire within and not beneath you can make it easier for you to overcome challenges and achieve long-term success.

One of the best decisions you will make in your lifetime is to consciously and diligently stand guard over the door of your heart as though you get paid for it.

Call to Action

- ◊ Create a list of facts and myths about your family or background, as you can recall.
- ◊ Highlight what you think has kept you stuck, write out all that God says about you and compare them. Now, consciously cross out every limiting belief on the list.
- ◊ List the people who positively influence you, believe in you, and support your goals. Choose to surround yourself with them and reach out to them.
- ◊ Set specific, achievable goals for yourself and plan to achieve them. Break down this plan into small steps every day, no matter how insignificant they might initially seem
- ◊ Stand in front of the mirror and practice positive self-talk and affirmations to reinforce a positive mindset.

- CHAPTER TWO -

Making a Mountain out of Almost Nothing

"Nothing can resist the human will that will stake even its existence on its stated purpose."

Benjamin Disraeli

The early 1990s were tough for my family. Every citizen felt the crunch, although in varying degrees. It was the era of military dictatorship in Nigeria when the country had to grapple with strict sanctions from the international community against the gross violation of human rights, a downward economic turn, and dwindling wealth, amongst others.

At that time, the earnings from my dad's professional practice no longer catered to the family's growing needs, and my mom's wages were left unpaid for several months as a civil servant. Because of this, my dad decided it was best to relocate his professional practice to Lagos, a major commercial center in Nigeria. At the same time, my mom remained with my siblings and me in Abeokuta, aka Rock City. The sudden transition was uneventful for my dad, as both parents were born and raised in Lagos.

Back home, we adapted to the new life of being prudent, especially regarding our finances and other resources. At the same time, ad's absence left a vacuum; thus, I had to step in and assist my mom in tasks my dad would typically take the lead. I recall having to sometimes wake up in the middle of the night to stand in a long queue at gas stations to buy fuel during periods of gas scarcity; push-start the family car every morning due to the battery's health; learn how to cook meals over firewood; grind pepper with a stone; give my baby sister a piggyback ride as I took her to daycare in the opposite direction of our house before going to my school; and the likes.

Those days had a gloomy economic forecast such that I thought it would be impossible for things to turn around for the better. Amidst the uncertainties, there was never a time I saw my mom with a gloomy disposition. Instead, she refused to allow the storms of life to displace her, and my mom constantly explored different ideas, ways and possibilities of making more money.

One day she came up with the concept of a retail shop where she would sell everyday items that families needed. The idea was great, but the major challenge was raising sufficient capital. We had no money stacked up somewhere, nor were there any financial institutions willing to invest in such a business, at least not to our knowledge, in such economically precarious times.

Much to my surprise, my mom diligently prepared daily to launch the company as though she had some spare cash secretly stashed away. It did not matter whether it was during the day or late at night; she was deeply dedicated to planning for the business in advance. And each time I peeped into her notes, I was amazed at the level of faith she possessed. My mom had gigantic dreams for herself and her family — inspiring!

One day, she returned from the market with a hand-held black plastic bag in her right hand. At first, I thought it contained groceries, but as I leaned toward her to collect it and put the contents away, she held the bag tightly.

"Mom, what's inside the bag?" I inquired curiously.

She remained eerily silent for a few seconds. When she finally spoke, she gazed at my siblings and me, revealing that her small plastic bag contained the materials necessary to commence her retail business. I couldn't believe what I heard and expressed my skepticism aloud, thinking it was some joke.

However, her demeanor was severe, and she went to the dining room to showcase the items she had acquired on a portable refrigerator. As soon as I realized that the bag held small consumable items like snacks and toiletries, my heart sank, and I retreated to my room, tears welling in my eyes as I struggled to suppress my emotions throughout the day.

The following day, I asked her how much she had spent to purchase the items.

"I spent ₦30 (about $20 in today's currency value)," she quipped.

Once again, I was amazed, struggling to differentiate between reality and a dream. But as the days went by and the frequency of customers knocking on our door increased, I saw a glimmer of hope at the end of the tunnel.

What would your reaction be if I told you that from starting with a meager ₦30 showcasing a few items for sale on a refrigerator by the window side to converting our garage into a shop and moving to multiple stores around town, my mom built a thriving business against seemingly insurmountable odds?

I can best describe her remarkable story of overcoming challenges and achieving success as making a mountain out of almost nothing.

She was undoubtedly a woman of unwavering faith who refused to settle for mediocrity. She mastered the skill of keeping scarcity at arm's length, which enabled her to transform something seemingly insignificant into a substantial achievement. The values instilled in me by my mother were instrumental in shaping me into the person I am today, and their profound impact on my entire life is immeasurable.

Making an Audacious Move

In my opinion, one of the most captivating stories in the Bible is "The Parable of the Talents." This powerful narrative emphasizes the importance of taking action, no matter how small the steps may seem. Allow me to retell the story:

Before embarking on a long journey, a master gave some talents to three of his servants. To the first, he gave five talents; to the second, he gave two talents; and to the third, he gave one talent.

After his departure, the servant with five talents and the one with two talents traded their money and doubled their wealth. However, the servant with only one talent buried it in the ground instead of investing it.

When the master returned, he asked each servant to explain how they had managed their talents. The servant with five talents and the one with two talents proudly recounted their successes to the master.

"We have invested and doubled the talents you gave us, and here are the profits," they reported.

Making a Mountain out of Almost Nothing

The master commended them for their diligence and promised to reward them accordingly for their hard work.

During the reckoning, the servant with the one talent had no positive report. Instead, he complained bitterly about how the master was a harsh and wicked man.

When he finished, the master responded in Matthew 25:26-27, "You wicked, lazy servant! So you knew that I harvest where I have not sown and gather where I have not scattered seed? Well then, you should have put my money on deposit with the bankers, so that when I returned I would have received it back with interest." The master was disappointed in the servant's lack of initiative and negative attitude.

Consequently, he took one talent from the servant and gave it to the servant who had multiplied his five talents.

How many talents do you possess? These talents could be in the form of tools, resources, skills, or technical know-how. Are you using them efficiently and effectively, or do you complain and make excuses about your abilities? Are you blaming external factors instead of taking responsibility for your lack of progress?

The key to significant improvement in life lies in appreciating and making the most of what you already have. The servant with one talent needed to have recognized the importance of making astute moves with his meager resources and, as a result, lost everything.

If you have a prodigious talent for singing but are frequently absent from rehearsals, you'll likely lose your spot to a more diligent individual who shows up regularly. Regardless of gender, location, education, socio-economic status, or religious beliefs, you should utilize your talents and skills to their fullest potential.

Let me share a story with you.

In college, I befriended someone who had to leave high school unexpectedly. To start anew, my friend went to live with her older sister, who owned a retail store. I enjoyed hanging out with her at the store and eventually started helping her on some evenings. I soon realized she had a sales talent and could quickly sell almost anything to anyone. Her responsible demeanor made her stand out in the store.

Before long, I began considering the possibility of urging my friend to utilize her sales skills more meaningfully, as I believed that in the future, she would have to venture out on her own and pursue her path.

One day, we had an opportunity to have a meaningful conversation, and during our talk, my friend expressed her interest in learning how to make manually-pressed juice. I was thrilled to hear that she was taking steps toward starting her own business. Through her hard work and determination, she was able to generate income and become financially independent despite facing many challenges. Her positive attitude towards exploring possibilities instead of dwelling on limitations was crucial to her success.

My friend's success story reminds me of the famous saying that the ship of failure sails on a sea of excuses. It's essential to cultivate a culture of "no excuses" and putting to use the talents that God has blessed you with. It would help if you took decisive action to avoid becoming irrelevant. Refrain from treating every challenge as an insurmountable obstacle; don't sit idle when you should be spreading your wings and flying high. Believe that it's possible and take action to make it a reality.

Success in life requires continuous and effective action, regardless of the challenges that may arise. Take proactive steps towards your goals, utilizing the resources you have at your disposal. Over time, your efforts will be noticed by those around you, and some of them will provide the support you need to progress to the next level. Keep pushing forward, and don't give up on your dreams.

Imagine you aim to further your education by enrolling in a school but cannot afford the tuition. Don't let this setback stop you from taking action. Take a significant step by researching and making a list of schools that offer your intended course of study, along with the tuition costs. Be ready to share this information with anyone who inquires about your education plans. By doing this, you may receive helpful advice or even financial assistance from unexpected sources. Keep moving toward your goal, taking smaller steps first.

In addition, consider reaching out to the faculty and current students of the schools you are interested in, familiarizing yourself with the curricula of your desired programs, and studying related content. Doing so increases your chances of excelling and standing out from the crowd. Your passion, desire, and determination to succeed will become a powerful magnet that attracts success, and the odds will be in your favor. So, take action today and prove me wrong if you can.

Preparing to Take a Detour

Financial independence was one of the recurring, key themes my mom constantly rang in my ears. "Anyone who commits to becoming financially independent will live a life of freedom," she would always advise me. Initially, I struggled to comprehend the connection between financial independence and liberation. However, as I developed my critical thinking abilities, I understood that achieving financial independence offers a path to freedom.

So, while in college, I pondered ways to supplement the financial support my parents provided me. Although I was not born into a wealthy family, we were not destitute either. Nevertheless, I aspired to attain financial independence by the time I graduated.

Consequently, I took essential measures to work towards this objective.

To begin with, I brainstormed various concepts to kickstart my financial independence journey. However, I realized that I needed more capital upon evaluating their practicality. This predicament mirrored the situation my mother faced in the past. As a student, I did not have access to loans, and I could not rely on affluent family members for support. Even if I did have wealthy relatives, I would have been reluctant to seek their assistance since I knew my parents would object.

During one of my brainstorming sessions, I recollected a cordial relationship I had established with a lady who sold shoes and purses at a nearby open-air market where I often spent my school breaks. Her shop was adjacent to a payphone booth, and she would frequently allow people waiting in line or for their calls to rest in her store, sheltering them from the blistering sun. She would invite me to sit and wait my turn with a warm smile. Grateful, I would smile and respond with a heartfelt "Amen." as time passed, we conversed about various topics, and she took a liking to me, often encouraging me by saying, "Seun, you are a well-mannered child, and you will go far in life."

Considering the reasonable prices of the shoes and purses she sold, I decided to buy some items from her to test the market and establish a supplier relationship. Despite lacking the funds to purchase, I reasoned that there was no harm in asking and thus headed to her shop. Upon arriving, despite not having seen each other for a while, she greeted me warmly, offering me a seat and a refreshing glass of water.

"How is school going on for you?" she asked.

"School is going well, and I am already looking forward to graduating," I replied.

My response elicited laughter from both of us, mainly since there needed to be more certainty regarding when students attending public tertiary institutions in Nigeria would graduate at that time.

There was a negative comment that students commonly made during those days. "Your graduation year from a Nigerian public higher education institution is determined by 4 + x years, where x can be any whole number from 1 to 10 or even more," they would joke. Many students would laugh it off, despite the complex nature of the matter.

The reasoning behind this line was that public higher education institutions in Nigeria frequently experienced incessant strikes that often resulted in students being out of school for several months during the academic year. Naturally, some years were better than others, depending on the severity of the issues.

Following our discussion about school, our conversation naturally transitioned to the reason for my visit. I explained to the woman that I had seriously considered selling shoes and purses in school and asked if she would allow me to take some of her products without upfront payment. Her reaction and response left me speechless, as I was pleasantly surprised. The woman assured me that I could take as many shoes and purses as I wanted and that it was acceptable to bring her the money whenever I could.

Although I comprehended what she had just said, I couldn't believe my ears. I stood there in disbelief, wondering if she was genuinely willing to trust me completely. Before leaving my apartment, I had thought about this scenario, but I wasn't ready for her to offer me a blank check. She assured me she had faith in my integrity and wouldn't be offended even if I didn't meet her expectations. I was uncertain how to respond to her kindness but I thanked her profusely. I expressed my gratitude for her trust and explained that I only needed six pairs of shoes and a few purses to test the waters. She graciously agreed to my request.

In school, I successfully marketed the shoes and handbags to acquaintances and sold all the items within a few days. One of my friends in school even started helping me sell the wares to people in her network, making the experience even more enjoyable. The expertise of convincing others to buy from me was exciting, empowering, and fulfilling. It felt like I was finally enjoying the fruits of my labor, and I kept returning to the woman's shop to restock.

I planned to accumulate sufficient money to finance a bigger business idea. This idea involved traveling to Lagos to purchase customized shirts, outfits, and accessories not readily available in Rock City and reselling them on campus at affordable prices. The earnings from selling the shoes and purses were significant, so I committed myself to saving at least 50% of the profits.

Regularly traveling to Lagos was a challenging feat that required meticulous planning, given the considerable distance, poor road conditions, and safety issues. Hence, I resolved to accumulate adequate funds to purchase supplies in large quantities, thereby minimizing the number of trips necessary. Despite the obstacles, this endeavor proved fruitful and propelled me to surpass my financial goals.

Encountering the detour on my path to achieving my financial objective taught me that being well-prepared for a venture increases your capacity to adjust to unforeseen circumstances. Drawing from my mother's business expertise, I used the lessons learned as a guide to navigate my journey.

Consider this situation: You leave your house with the plan of taking a well-known path to the grocery store, only to discover that the road is closed halfway. This situation is akin to how unexpected detours present themselves in our lives. Life's obstacles can appear without warning, catching us off guard, but we can equip ourselves to handle them. Remember that the degree of preparation you undertake will aid you in navigating detours along your journey, allowing you to reach your desired destination or attain your objective without squandering time. If you aspire to overcome challenges and achieve significant success in life, you must be willing to take a detour when the need arises.

Keeping the Dream Alive

At ten, I discovered that writing brought me immense joy. I developed a fondness for crafting stories that conveyed valuable life lessons. Writing remains my method of escaping from a noisy world and serves as a channel for expressing my ideas purposefully and rewardingly.

I wrote my debut book, "Tunde Goes to School," about a young boy who lost his parents at a tender age and had to reside with his aunt, who couldn't afford to send him to school. The protagonist, Tunde, a young orphan, faced severe hardships until he crossed paths with a new family. In exchange for funding his secondary school education, Tunde agreed to work for them. Upon finishing the book, I stashed it under my bed, too apprehensive to reveal it.

One Saturday morning, while performing her daily house cleaning, my mother stumbled upon the book and was amazed at my ingenuity.

"When did you write this?" she inquired, holding the book in clear sight for me to see.

"I wrote it every night, Mom," I replied, anxious.

In those days, it was challenging to anticipate my mother's reaction to particular circumstances. She probed further, inquiring about my plans for the book.

"What do you intend to do with the book?" she asked firmly.

"It would be my greatest pleasure if the book could be published," I said, hoping for a positive response.

My mother smiled and spoke at length about our family's inability to publish the book then.

"Maybe we can reconsider the idea once you graduate high school," she suggested.

I was immensely disheartened, and my countenance immediately revealed my despondency. My aspiration of becoming a published author appeared to be slipping through my fingers, yet I persisted in holding onto hope.

From my college days until my marriage, I was preoccupied with various obligations, leaving me with no option but to temporarily sideline my aspirations of becoming a published author. Upon my high school graduation, I composed several other books but kept them to myself. Given their other pressing responsibilities, I refrained from burdening my parents with the prospect of publishing my work.

Despite my busy schedule during those years, I persisted in jotting down my musings on various life topics. And as the internet became increasingly accessible to a broader audience, I saw a glimmer of hope in sharing my ideas with the world.

In 2013, I stumbled upon blogging as a platform to express my thoughts. Since then, I have published various articles, from personal growth and leadership to business, careers, marriage, and financial independence. As a result of this endeavor, I became a published author. I acquired the opportunity to teach, speak, coach, and mentor individuals from diverse parts of the world - a privilege I continue to relish.

As you journey through life, you may encounter situations where your dreams seem to be slipping away, not because of your negligence but due to circumstances beyond your control. In such moments, it is essential to remember that "delay is not denial." Although it is easy to say, implementing this philosophy can be challenging. However, your attitude and actions when faced with unexpected setbacks will determine whether or not your dreams will eventually become a reality.

A great example is Joseph from the Bible, who had childhood dreams of ruling over his family. Unexpected setbacks and delays threatened the possibility of his dreams becoming a reality, but eventually, they did come true. Similarly, your dreams are valid and can become a reality if you persist in pursuing them, no matter the obstacles.

Call to Action

◊ Reflect on a recent change in your life and brainstorm five strategies to adapt.

◊ Take strategic actions to pursue your goals and avoid being hindered by financial limitations. Look for creative ways to overcome financial barriers and seek opportunities to advance toward your desired outcomes. Remember that determination and resourcefulness can help you overcome obstacles and achieve success.

◊ In what ways have you demonstrated belief in yourself and unwavering faith in your abilities? Jot them down.

◊ Recognize and appreciate the skills, talents, tools, resources, and technical knowledge you possess now, and actively seek opportunities to utilize them. Start small with what you have and gradually grow more prominent. Take the first step towards this by writing down a plan to maximize your current resources and work towards achieving your goals.

- CHAPTER THREE -

Gaining Clarity

"The greater clarity you have about who you are and what you want, the more you will achieve and the faster you will achieve it in every area of your life."

Brian Tracy

During my senior year of high school, many of us participated in a popular activity, filling out "slum books." These books were like a manual version of today's Facebook, where we shared our goals, dreams, aspirations, and personal lives. Unlike today's digital text, we use pencils and pens to write them. Reading through the filled-out pages and learning more about our peers was always enjoyable.

Whenever I received a slum book to fill, I eagerly anticipated the question, "What is your future career?" I consistently answered, "I aspire to have a medical career." I wanted to become a medical doctor not because I thought it was God's purpose for me but because my desire was borne out of the fact that ever since I was a child, everything about my journey, including my affinity for science-related subjects, seemed to suggest that I would inevitably become a doctor. So, when it was time for me to choose a career path during my transition into senior secondary school, I opted for the sciences pathway.

My vision of becoming a medical doctor was deeply ingrained in my mind during those years. I was resolute, and no one could sway me from my goal. I was determined to overcome any obstacle that may come my way in achieving my dream. I took several exams to reach my career aspirations, including the University Matriculation Examination (UME) administered by The Joint Admissions and Matriculation Board (JAMB).

As a prospect to receive an offer of admission to a medical school outside of Rock City, I eagerly awaited the results after taking multiple exams and began making plans to relocate from Rock City. Being in the same place for so long made me yearn for a fresh start and a broader life experience that college years outside of Rock City could offer.

As I planned to relocate from Rock City, the long-awaited UME results were finally released. News of the release quickly spread around town, and I eagerly awaited my results. At the time, you had to visit the UME Office to view your results physically, so my mother went to collect them on my behalf. To my great disappointment, my scores were below the cut-off for admission into the medical schools I had chosen. I was devastated and wept uncontrollably for several days. I insisted for a while that there must have been an error somewhere.

Before my UME results, I had always been a high achiever and couldn't remember when I failed at any subject, even the more challenging ones. Failing to meet the required cumulative mark for medical school admission was a devastating blow that left me feeling like I had let down my entire community and caused my world to crumble beneath my feet. However, my mother recognized my despair and encouraged me that there would always be opportunities for a retake as long as I had a life.

The UME was an annual exam, so while my peers who scored high enough for their desired courses were off to college, I had to wait at home for a year to retake the exam. The thought of being left behind did not sit well with me, but I found solace in God's promises in the Bible and the support of my dear teachers, friends, and family members.

A Moment of Confusion

I purchased a new UME Application Form the following year with the support of my parents and enrolled in a private tutoring center to improve my chances of achieving a better score. While preparing for the examinations, my mother came home from work one day and suggested that "pharmacy" could be a better course for me to study. I was taken aback and asked, "Pharmacy?"

> "Yes, pharmacy is a great course, and I believe you would excel as a pharmacist," she replied.

I began considering the possibility of becoming a pharmacist after my mother suggested it, and the idea started to take hold. However, before I could fully embrace this new path, my mother introduced the idea of becoming a geologist. She explained the benefits of studying geology in college, even though I wasn't entirely sure what it entailed. Despite my uncertainty, I was open to exploring this potential career path.

To add to the information overload, my mother frequently came home from work and suggested new courses of study she had discovered and why I should consider them. The back and forth went on for about three months, and I felt like a dice tossed from one end of the board to another. Ultimately, I didn't pursue a medical or pharmacy degree, or any of the other courses suggested to me. Surprisingly, I eventually settled on studying environmental management and toxicology at the University of Agriculture, Alabata, Ogun State, Nigeria.

How can one go from wanting to study medicine and surgery to becoming a toxicology student? The honest answer lies in these three words: lack of clarity.

Yes, it was true. Everything about my journey at the time pointed to me pursuing a career as a medical professional. Still, I needed more clarity about why I wanted to become a medical doctor. If I had a clear conviction about the choice to become a medical doctor, it would have been an uphill task for anyone to talk me out of it. I would have stood my ground when other people's suggestions that were out of alignment with my dreams were rammed down my throat. Rather than being drawn into a situation divergent from what I wanted to be initially, I would have remained focused and resolute in pursuing my goals.

In the end, I decided to pursue environmental management and toxicology based on my personal conviction and today, I have no regrets or bitterness about my decision. The same cannot be said of many others who were in my shoes at that time. I attended college with many students who had no input in choosing their course of study nor did they have a clear picture of where they were headed.

Lack of clarity often leads to confusion and settling for things contrary to your intention. Knowing what you want is essential to achieve your desired goals. When you clearly understand what you want, you can overcome life's challenges and live the life of your dreams. This clarity will also help you maintain your balance and focus, even when others try to push you off course.

In his book, "Put Your Dreams to the Test," John C. Maxwell stated, "If you want to accomplish a dream, you will be able to do so when you can see it. It would help if you defined it before you can pursue it. Most people do not do that. Their dreams remain a dream — something fuzzy and unspecific. As a result, they never achieve it." Without clarity, your journey and destination will lack direction and purpose, leading to stagnation instead of progress. It's essential to gain clarity to move forward toward achieving your goals.

Why Clarity Is Important

Clarity is crucial for success, no matter where you are. You must be clear about your goals, dreams, and desires to succeed. Having clarity will help you move forward in the direction of your aspirations. Here are some critical reasons why clarity is a constant essential for success.

◊ **Clarity helps you save time:** Having clarity in your goals, desires, and priorities can help you save time by allowing you to focus your efforts and energies on what truly matters. When you know your goals, you can create a clear plan of action and eliminate any unnecessary tasks or distractions. For instance, if your goal is to start a business, having clarity about the type of business you want to run, the target market, and the resources required will enable you to prioritize tasks that will move you closer to achieving your goal. You will be less likely to waste time on activities that do not align with your objectives.

Moreover, clarity can help you make better decisions in less time. When clear about what you want, you will likely be more confident about the best course of action. Having clarity saves time and reduces the stress that comes with decision-making. For example, if you are clear about your career goals, you can quickly evaluate job offers and make informed decisions about which opportunities align with your aspirations. Clarity can help you use your time more efficiently and effectively, allowing you to achieve your goals and live a fulfilling life.

⋄ **Clarity helps you save money and resources:** Having clarity can also help you save money and resources in various ways. When you are clear about what you want, you are less likely to waste money on unnecessary purchases. For example, if you are clear about your financial goals, you will be less likely to make impulsive purchases that do not align with those goals. Clarity can help you save money in the long run and use your resources more efficiently. Additionally, having clarity can help you prioritize your spending and invest in things that are truly important to you, helping you make better financial decisions and avoid wasting money on things that do not bring you value or joy.

Clarity can help you work more efficiently and effectively, reducing the amount of time and energy you need to achieve your goals. Furthermore, having clarity can also help you save resources in terms of time and energy. When you clearly understand what you want, you can focus your time and energy on achieving those goals and avoid wasting them on distractions or activities that do not contribute to your success. Additionally, having clarity can help you identify opportunities to streamline your processes and optimize your use of resources, such as automating tasks or outsourcing non-essential activities. When you are clear about your goals, you save time, energy, and money in the long run, allowing you to achieve your goals more quickly and easily.

⋄ **Clarity assists you in pursuing your goals with conviction:** Have you ever wondered why it seems like some people know how to pursue their goals with utter confidence? It is because such people have gained clarity!

Clarity is such a powerful force that propels people toward their dreams.

When my childhood friend, Capt. Abimbola Jayeola decided it was time to go to an aviation school in steadfast pursuit of her dreams of becoming a pilot; she was already in graduate school and on the way to being a college professor. All that changed the moment she became crystal clear about her goals. It did not matter the types of opposition or resistance from those around her; she pursued her dream of becoming a pilot with conviction and became the first female helicopter pilot in Nigeria.

Clarity about your goals provides a sense of direction and purpose, which in turn helps you pursue them with conviction. When you clearly understand what you want to achieve, you can create an action plan and take specific steps toward your goal. With clarity, you can prioritize your tasks and time, maximizing every opportunity to work towards your goal. This focus and determination will help you stay motivated and overcome any obstacles that may come your way.

Also, having clarity can help you identify the resources and support you need to achieve your goals. When you are clear about your goals and why they matter to you, it becomes easier to communicate your vision to others and seek their help. You can contact mentors, peers, and other experts in your field who can offer guidance, support, and resources to help you achieve your goals. This collaborative effort can help you pursue your goals with more confidence and conviction, knowing that you have the backing of others who believe in you and your vision.

◊ **Clarity makes people support you:** When you are clear about your goals, there is a different aura around you that signals to people that you know what you want.

Having clarity attracts people who can support you in achieving your goals.

I once met a young woman who wanted to scale her business, and by the time I spent 15 minutes with her, I could perceive that she was unsure of what she wanted to do. People often think they have dreams when, in fact, what they have is an illusion. An illusion is unreal or fuzzy, and it lacks definition. You must gain clarity if you want people to support you in achieving your goals.

Clarity about your goals and aspirations can make it easier for others to support you because they will clearly understand what you are trying to achieve. People who understand your goals are more willing to offer their time, resources, and connections to help you succeed. For example, if you are trying to start a business and communicate your vision, mission, and goals to potential investors, they will likely support you with funding and guidance. Similarly, suppose you are trying to advance in your career, and you communicate your goals to your colleagues. In that case, they may be more willing to provide mentorship, introductions, and other forms of support.

Furthermore, clarity can make it easier for others to understand your goals, leading to increased support. When people understand your goals and the impact they can have, they are more likely to rally behind you and help you achieve success. For example, suppose you are working on a project to promote sustainable living and communicate your work's environmental and social benefits. In that case, people who care about those issues may be more likely to support you with their time, money, and other resources.

◊ **Clarity guides you in charting the right course:** Clarity is necessary to chart a course. But with clarity, you can chart the right path and increase your chances of reaching your destination.

When I first joined my previous organization, one of my duties was to conduct a thorough inspection at different regulatory sites. At that time, I had not fully grasped the importance of having clarity in all aspects of life. For instance, I would set out to visit at least three sites and end the day without reaching any. I often drove completely off course because I needed clarification about where I was headed. It took me a while to understand that things do not just fall in place because I expect them to but because I am clear about where I want them to fall. If you genuinely want to become a success anywhere you find yourself, you must be clear on your dreams, goals and aspirations.

◊ **Clarity inspires action:** Clarity spurs you to take action and action drives results! You have access to this book because you have gained clarity. You understand the importance of personal development, have set clear goals, and are now in the action phase. For example, writing a book is an activity that could easily fall through the cracks, but because I was clear on my book-writing book goal, I was inspired to act against all odds. You need to be clear about your goals before you feel like it is impossible to achieve them. And once you fail to work when you are supposed to, you may become complacent to the point that the dream will never become a reality.

Steps to Gaining Clarity

Gaining clarity in life can be an ongoing process, but taking specific steps can help you move toward a clearer understanding of your goals, values, and aspirations. Whether you want clarity in your career, relationships, or personal growth, there are practical steps to clarify your vision and progress toward the life you want to live. Here are some effective strategies and practices for gaining clarity and taking action towards your desired outcomes you can explore.

◊ **Take Time to Meditate:** Achieving what you want in life requires a calm and clear mind, especially when progress is slow. Stress and anxiety can cloud your thoughts, making it difficult to have clarity and focus on your goals. Therefore, taking care of your mental health and well-being is essential to keep a clear and focused mind.

I maintain a clear and focused mind by meditating on God's words in the Bible. How about you? Meditation can be a powerful tool for clarifying what truly matters in your life.

By sitting in silence and observing your thoughts and emotions, you can become more aware of your deepest values and desires. This heightened awareness can help you align your goals with your purpose, values, and God's desire for you, ultimately leading to greater fulfillment and achievement.

In addition to gaining clarity about your goals, meditation can help you develop the qualities needed to achieve them. Building sustained effort, patience, and persistence are critical to realizing meaningful goals, and meditation can be a valuable tool in cultivating these qualities. By teaching you to live in the moment and accept things as they are rather than constantly striving for immediate results, meditation can help you stay focused and motivated on your path to success.

Therefore, create time for meditation and make it a habit by practicing it often because you need to clarify your intentions, stay focused, manage stress and anxiety, and develop patience and persistence. These are key to making your dreams come true.

◊ **Write Down Your Goals:** My mom first taught me the power of writing down my goals. I grew up watching my mom always pen down her goals, which helped her diligently pursue them. Even for tasks that many people considered mundane back then, such as going to the grocery store, my mom had the habit of writing down exactly what she intended to purchase.

I picked up this habit from her, which has helped me achieve more than I would ever attain without writing down my goals. Also, as I began to invest in personal development, I learned more about the importance of writing down my goals, including how to create vision boards for different aspects of my life. Vision boards serve as a powerful tool for visualization that has helped me to gain clarity in many facets of my life, making me feel like I am in control of my destiny in the long run.

In 2016 I decided to organize an event centered on creating effective vision boards where I taught attendees how they could make theirs. The valuable feedback I received encouraged me to turn that into an annual event. Many people who attended the first edition still show up at this event to date. If you do not have one or are reading about it for the first time, learn how to create and make your vision board.

Writing down your goals is crucial to gaining clarity as it helps you articulate what you genuinely want to achieve. By putting your thoughts down on paper, you create a clear picture of your aspirations, which makes it easier to develop a plan of action. For instance, if your goal is to start a business, writing it down will help you clarify what type of business you want to start, who your target audience is, and what steps you need to take to make your business idea a reality.

In addition, writing down your goals can help you prioritize your objectives and identify the ones most important to you. You can also break down your long-term goals into smaller, more manageable tasks, making tracking your progress and staying motivated easier. For example, suppose you want to run a marathon. In that case, you can break down your training into smaller goals, such as running a certain number of miles weekly, increasing your speed gradually, and incorporating strength training into your routine.

Writing your goals can help you stay focused and motivated even when you face obstacles or setbacks. Furthermore, writing down your goals can also help you stay accountable. Once you have written your goals, you can refer to them regularly to remind yourself what you want to achieve. You can also share your goals with a trusted friend or family member who can help keep you accountable and support you in achieving your aspirations.

◊ **Start Doing:** After writing down your goals; the next step is to take action toward achieving them. Waiting for the perfect conditions before you start may hinder your progress, and you may never get started. By taking action, you gain clarity on what works and does not. You can then adjust your approach accordingly and make progress towards your goals.

I recall the remarkable story of a renowned baker based in Lagos, Nigeria, who had a clear vision of building a bakery brand with numerous outlets but lacked the resources to bring her dream to fruition. However, instead of waiting idly for the capital she believed she needed, she took a proactive approach. She began baking in her kitchen before leaving for her day job, where she fulfilled her responsibilities with dedication and diligence. She devoted two to three hours in the evenings to fulfilling customers' orders before retiring for the night. This routine continued for eight years until she eventually left her paid employment to start her own business. Today, her bakery has expanded to more than eight locations in Nigeria, with over 100 employees.

Can you imagine if she had waited until everything was set? Perhaps, today, she'd still be waiting. It is crucial to keep things in motion to achieve success and gain clarity. The more you take action, the more precise your path becomes and the closer you reach your goals. Refrain from letting the lack of resources or waiting for the perfect time hold you back. Take the first step towards your goal today, and keep moving forward. Whether starting a new project, learning a new skill, or launching a business idea, every action counts towards creating the life you want. Remember that progress, no matter how small, is still progress.

◊ **Have an Accountability Partner:** There are instances where our ideas may need more clarity once we engage in discussions with others. In 2015 when I was considering organizing an empowerment program, I saw the benefit of an accountability partner. Despite having a general idea of wanting to do something related to women's empowerment, I was still determining how to execute it. The lack of clarity left me feeling unsure and stuck.

One day, while feeling lost and uncertain about how to run my plan for an empowerment program, I talked with a friend who also serves as my accountability partner. I spoke to her during a meeting about my aspirations, and she provided me with valuable insight and guidance. As we discussed my ideas, they became more evident, and I felt the missing pieces of my goals were falling into place. With her encouragement and support, I was able to host a successful conference that remains one of the best decisions I have ever made.

Having an accountability partner is a powerful tool for gaining clarity and achieving success. This story is an excellent example of how discussing your goals with someone you trust can help you gain the clarity and direction you need. It is essential to choose an accountability partner who is trustworthy, supportive, and secure in their calling. You want to share your dreams with someone who genuinely desires your success and will provide constructive feedback and encouragement.

You can gain the clarity and motivation to realize your dreams with the right accountability partner.

Call to Action

◊ If you still need to take the time to reflect on your goals, vision, and aspirations, it is crucial to do so. One effective way to clarify your thoughts is to write them down in specific words. This writing process can help you organize your thoughts, prioritize your goals, and develop a clear plan of action to achieve them. It is essential to be specific when writing down your goals, including timelines, resources, and the steps required to achieve them. By doing this, you can create a roadmap to guide you toward success.

◊ Choose to remain unwavering and committed to achieving your dreams, despite distractions and obstacles. Ditch any ideas or suggestions that do not align with your ultimate vision for your life.

◊ To gain clarity and stay on track toward your goals, seeking guidance and advice from trusted sources can be helpful. Be sure to choose people with experience and expertise in the areas you need help with and who you trust to give you honest and constructive feedback.

◊ Take time to meditate, and make it a daily routine.

◊ Get an accountability partner who has your best interests at heart and wants you to succeed.

◊ Create a vision board. It is an effective tool for visualization.

- CHAPTER FOUR -

Catapulting into the Limelight

"The heights that great men reached and kept were not attained by sudden flight, but they, while their companions slept, were toiling upward in the night."

Henry Wadsworth Longfellow

On January 15, 2009, US Airways Flight 1549, en route from LaGuardia Airport, New York City, to Charlotte Douglas International Airport, Charlotte, North Carolina, as the stopover but bound for Seattle-Tacoma International Airport, Seattle, Washington, with 155 people aboard the flight ditched in the Hudson River off Midtown Manhattan of New York City. To the wide-eyed amazement of millions who watched worldwide, everyone made it out alive, staving off what could have been an enormous, devastating loss of lives! After returning from work, I did something unusual on that fateful day and turned on the television to catch up with the news. Typically, watching TV on weekdays was not my habit. As I went about my chores in different parts of the house, I overheard a news reporter broadcasting about an incident in New York City involving a plane carrying many passengers. To this day, I cannot explain why I felt compelled to tune in.

"Not again!" I exclaimed as I hurriedly made my way to the living room. Upon getting there, I watched in awe, on live television, as the emergency officials rescued passengers from the slightly submerged airplane. It felt like I was in a dream as every passenger walked away from the scene unscathed. That unexpected yet miraculous outcome turned the captain and pilot in command of the aircraft, Chesley Sullenberger — an obscure pilot — into a highly celebrated personality overnight. His act of bravery, calmness in a terrifying situation, and extraordinary ability to act with precision when it mattered most earned him a notable spot in the Hall of Fame in organizations across the United States of America and indeed around the world.

After witnessing a series of interview sessions with Captain Sullenberger in the aftermath of the incident, my interest was piqued, and I felt compelled to dig even deeper. I was determined to uncover the secret behind his remarkable display of skill and bravery. Through my research, I discovered Captain Sullenberger had been diligent and dedicated to his career since childhood. At the time of the incident, reports indicated that he had accumulated 19,663 flight hours over 40 years.

Following takeoff from the airport, the Airbus A320 serving the flight was reportedly hit by a flock of Canada geese, resulting in a loss of engine power. In a split-second, life-or-death decision, the captain was faced with attempting an emergency landing in a densely populated neighborhood or ditching the plane in the Hudson River. The captain chose to perform the latter, successfully executing the landing and saving the lives of all passengers and crew onboard. This incredible feat has been dubbed the "Miracle on the Hudson."

That day's events forever changed Captain Sully's life trajectory, propelling him from a relatively unknown aviator to a globally recognized and respected figure. Following the successful emergency landing of US Airways Flight 1549, Sully began to receive invitations for interviews and speaking engagements, and he was recognized with numerous awards for his heroic actions. The crowning achievement of his newfound fame came in 2016 with the release of a dramatic film titled "Sully," based on his memoir titled "Highest Duty: My Search for What Really Matters." The film chronicled the events of the Miracle on the Hudson and Sully's role in safely landing the plane in the Hudson River. Through this film, Sully's remarkable story reached an even wider audience, cementing his place in aviation history and inspiring countless individuals worldwide.

Becoming an Overnight Success

Suppose you were to only hear about Capt. Sully's incredible achievement, without delving into the years of preparation and training that led up to it, you may believe that he became an overnight success. However, if you understand the dedication and hard work required to succeed in any field, you will know that preparation always precedes elevation.

I vividly remember attending a business development event in Philadelphia about a decade ago when I had just begun cultivating the habit of attending paid events. Before that day, I would decline invitations to events that required payment, using the excuse that I couldn't afford it. But as soon as I arrived at the venue, I was struck by an overwhelming sense of satisfaction. The event's ambiance, registration materials, and attendees' faces impressed me. I eagerly awaited the convener's welcome address.

The program began promptly, and the time arrived for the host to address the audience. With thunderous applause, she began, "I am a 19-year overnight success." She described the trials and tribulations it took to achieve the desired success. She recounted being repeatedly overlooked for opportunities, her experience starting a business with an employee who then absconded with all of her customers' information, and how she became homeless. She also shared how she rebuilt her business from scratch. By the end of her address, not only did her story resonate with me, but it also reminded me of my mother, who, despite losing two of her stores to a road expansion project, managed to reinvent herself against all odds.

Preparation Precedes Success

My body grew astonishingly during my early teenage years, so I was already towering over most of my classmates when I entered high school. My height was such a notable feature that my peers called me "omo ga," which roughly translates to "the tall child" in my native language. While it was a lighthearted moniker, it also made me feel somewhat self-conscious, as I couldn't help but feel like I stood out from the crowd exaggeratedly. Nonetheless, I learned to embrace my height and recognize it as a part of my unique identity.

In a community where academic success was highly valued, extracurricular activities provided a refreshing change of pace. One day, the school administrators planned to organize an in-house sports competition. The announcement of the school's upcoming in-house sports competition was met with excitement by most students, myself included.

I had always been drawn to military parades and the precision that came with them, so I thought that would be the perfect activity for me to participate in. However, many people commented on how my long legs would be an asset in athletics, and this piqued my interest. After some consideration, I decided to compete in the 200-meter race, hoping to utilize my physical advantage to excel.

As the inter-house sports day approached, volunteer instructors stepped forward to organize and train the students who wanted to participate in the event. Determined to excel in the 200-meter race, I attended several practice drills. However, it soon became evident that I needed more than my long legs to guarantee success. I was out of form, my pace was slow, and I barely managed to cross the finish line during practice.

Despite my lackluster performance, the instructor kept asking me about my strategy for the upcoming competition. I always replied with the same vague answer, "I got it." However, deep down, I knew that simply relying on my physical attributes without doing the necessary work was a recipe for disaster.

The thought of practicing at home occasionally crossed my mind, but other tasks and activities often pull me in different directions. Despite acknowledging the importance of practice, I needed help to prioritize it. Though disappointed in my inability to practice, I continued to believe that my natural abilities would kick in when I needed them the most and that I would emerge victorious on the day of the competition.

On the event day, I arrived at school early, eager to give myself an edge. I wanted to compensate for lost time and ensure my chances of winning the 200-meter race. As I tested the tracks, I felt optimistic, believing that my long legs would give me the needed advantage. However, as the race began, my confidence shattered as I realized my legs were not carrying me as fast as I had hoped. Despite my height, I could not produce the results I had envisioned. It was a painful lesson learned, as I finished last in the race. I watched in awe as the other participants, who had prepared consistently and adequately, passed me quickly. They had trained hard, regardless of their height, and their efforts paid off. At that moment, I realized that success is not guaranteed solely by natural talents or advantages but is achieved through diligent and consistent preparation.

It is crucial to understand that possessing a desirable quality is not enough to guarantee success, as I learned from my experience of participating in the 200-meter race at school. Although having long legs seemed like an advantage for an athlete, it was not sufficient to win the race. Because of this, I missed the opportunity to become an outstanding athlete at school. I made the mistake of relying solely on my physical attributes and failed to combine them with hard work, preparation, and consistency, which are the keys to success.

Brian Tracy, a renowned motivational speaker and author of "Goals!: How to Get Everything You Want-Faster Than You Ever Thought Possible," rightly emphasized the importance of proper prior planning for success. In the book, he notes that "Proper Prior Planning Prevents Poor Performance," which he considers to be the formula for personal and business success. I wholeheartedly agree with him. Therefore, it is essential to prioritize preparation and consistency to achieve one's goals and avoid making the same mistake I made.

Capt. Sully's Model for Success

Capt. Sully is a person who has greatly inspired me and continues to do so. I am drawn to his maturity, diligence, and resoluteness toward the things he believes in. He dedicated himself to honing his skills and perfecting his craft until he was called upon to showcase his abilities. The biblical David exhibited this same level of dedication and preparation. As a shepherd boy, he focused on developing his life-saving skills long before he had to confront Goliath. According to the Bible, David could kill a bear and a lion with his bare hands, a feat that required significant investments in his skills and abilities.

In both cases, Capt. Sully and David understood the importance of preparation and consistently working on their craft. They started developing their skills before they had to confront a crisis. Instead, they took proactive steps to establish themselves to excel when the time came. This is a valuable lesson for all of us, personally or professionally. Investing in our skills, consistently working on our craft, and being prepared for any challenge that comes our way is the key to success.

As I write this book, there is no way I can determine where you are in life's journey, but I am sure there's always room for improvement. You can make a big difference over time by making small, consistent improvements to your approach, attitude, and outlook on life. This will ensure that you'll be fully prepared to make an impact when your time comes.

Have you invested enough in yourself? Are your skills fully developed, or are they still half-baked? How do you approach life's challenges? These are essential questions to consider as they will determine your level of success. Take the time to invest in yourself, hone your skills, and adopt a positive attitude toward life. Doing so will set you on the path to success.

Next, carefully consider these three tips and work on them:

a.) Sharpen your skills in obscurity: To succeed in life, it is vital to think and strategize, but it is equally important to get your hands dirty and work hard in obscurity. This involves putting in the necessary effort to hone your skills and abilities, even when nobody is watching. By doing so, you can avoid distractions and prepare yourself for the opportunities that will eventually come your way. When the time comes for you to shine, you will be fully equipped and ready to showcase your skills and abilities to the world. Remember, success is not just about talent or luck but also about consistent hard work and preparation.

b.) See challenges as opportunities: If you seek greatness, it's time to embrace challenges rather than run away from them. Challenges present opportunities for character-building, problem-solving, and skill enhancement. They are the stepping stones to personal growth and development.

Overcoming challenges builds resilience and mental toughness, which are crucial for success in any field. By facing and conquering obstacles, you will gain confidence in your abilities and develop a sense of self-efficacy that will propel you toward achieving your goals. Challenges also provide opportunities to sharpen your problem-solving skills. This will set you apart from others who shy away from challenges and lack the skills to tackle complex problems. You will learn to think creatively and develop innovative solutions when encountering obstacles and setbacks.

As you evolve, remember that challenges are not to be feared but embraced. They are the crucibles that will refine you and bring out the best in you. So, the next time you face a challenge, don't run away from it; embrace it as an opportunity to grow and become great.

c.) Be patient: Achieving success is not an overnight process; it requires patience and perseverance. Captain Sully's journey to success took 40 years of hard work and dedication, a testament to the fact that success is a gradual and continuous process. It is essential to understand that there may be setbacks and failures along the way, but these should not discourage you from pursuing your goals. Instead, view them as learning opportunities and use them to improve your approach.

It is crucial to refrain from comparing your progress with that of others. Or measuring success solely by external factors such as material possessions or social status is vital. Instead, I recommend you focus on your personal growth and development and take pride in your progress, no matter how small. With patience, persistence, and a positive attitude, your hard work and dedication will pay off in due time, and you will achieve your desired success.

Achieving Success with Limited Resources

A few years ago, during a mentorship session I organized for some of my protégés, one of them posed a question about achieving success despite limited access to resources that could propel her into the limelight. She lived in a country where it was difficult to access the Internet due to poor infrastructure, ineffective government policies, and limited resources. Drawing from my experience of overcoming challenges and achieving many of my goals with little to no help, I shared some strategies with her.

When advising my protégé on achieving success despite limited access to resources, I stressed the importance of focusing on mindset. While we may not have control over our family background, country of origin, or gender, we control our beliefs, attitude, and goals. By shifting her mindset from limitation to possibility, she could begin to see opportunities where others only saw obstacles.

I encouraged her to adopt a growth mindset and to view challenges as opportunities for learning and growth. Rather than seeing her lack of resources as a barrier to success, she could view it as a challenge to be creative and resourceful. Adopting this mindset would make her better equipped to find innovative solutions to her challenges. I also emphasized the importance of setting achievable goals and taking consistent action. With limited resources, it is easy to become overwhelmed and discouraged. However, she could build momentum and make steady progress by breaking her goals into small, manageable steps and taking consistent action.

To achieve success despite limited resources, one must shift their focus from the scarcity of resources to personal growth and development. This involves actively seeking opportunities to learn new skills, acquire knowledge, and enhance your abilities. The Internet is a valuable tool for accessing online courses and resources that can help you develop yourself. Adopting an attitude that facilitates learning, regardless of your circumstances, is essential.

Many online learning platforms, like Coursera, provide courses in high-demand skills, such as programming, marketing, and design. By investing your time and effort into these courses, you can gain the skills to start a business, freelance, or provide valuable services to others. However, it's essential to acknowledge that access to the Internet might only sometimes be readily available, and you might have to save money to afford Internet data services.

Choosing to save money for internet access is a sacrifice that will consistently benefit you in the future. Investing in yourself and developing your skills increases your chances of success, regardless of your resources. Remember, success is not determined solely by your resources but by your ability to utilize them effectively.

As you strive to acquire new skills and knowledge, you must also focus on building relationships and networking with others. History has shown that no outstanding achievement was accomplished alone. Stepping outside your comfort zone may be difficult, but connecting with others can lead to new opportunities. Through networking, I have met outstanding individuals who have needed my skills and expertise, leading to countless opportunities. Similarly, you should seek to connect with others in your industry or field. By expanding your network, you increase your chances of achieving success, as there are individuals who are strategically placed in your sphere of influence to offer support, guidance, and opportunities. Cultivating relationships with those who believe in your vision can be crucial to success, even with limited resources.

How do you get to network?

Networking can be a powerful tool for achieving success with limited resources, but it's essential to approach it with the right mindset. Online and offline networking can be effective, and there are various ways to get involved. Joining online communities or groups relevant to your interests or industry can give you access to a network of like-minded people. Attending events, conferences, and seminars can also be an opportunity to meet new people and establish connections. Social media platforms such as LinkedIn, Twitter, and Instagram can also be used for networking purposes.

However, it's important to remember that networking isn't just about what you can get from others and what you can offer them. Approaching networking to give value to others rather than just for selfish reasons can be more effective in building long-term relationships. Providing value can take many forms, such as sharing knowledge, offering services, or providing referrals. By doing this, you can establish yourself as a valuable resource to others and potentially open up new opportunities for yourself in the future.

Another strategy for achieving success with limited resources is being resourceful. This requires finding creative solutions to problems and utilizing the available resources. For instance, if you face financial constraints, you can explore alternative financing options such as crowdfunding or micro-loans to secure funding for your project. Similarly, if formal education is out of reach, you can seek mentorship or apprenticeship opportunities to learn on the job and acquire practical skills.

Being resourceful entails looking beyond your current limitations and finding innovative ways to achieve your goals. This may involve thinking outside the box, being open to new ideas, and utilizing your creativity. When you are resourceful, you do not allow the lack of resources to hinder your progress. Instead, you leverage your resources and make the most of them to succeed. This can include leveraging your network, bartering services, or using free online resources to gain knowledge and develop new skills. Being resourceful makes you better equipped to overcome obstacles and achieve your desired success.

Lastly, having a clear vision and focus is crucial to achieving success with limited resources. Knowing what you want to achieve and remaining dedicated to that goal can provide direction and purpose. It also helps you prioritize your actions and maximize your available resources. Distractions can derail your progress, so staying focused is critical.

But, more than having a clear vision and focus is required. Perseverance is also essential. The journey to success can be challenging sailing. You will face setbacks, obstacles, and failures along the way. However, perseverance helps you to keep going and overcome challenges. The more you persevere, the higher your chances of achieving success.

It's important to note that perseverance doesn't mean mindlessly pushing forward without evaluating and adjusting your strategies. It's about persisting while making necessary adjustments and learning from your failures. With determination, you can turn obstacles into opportunities and reach your goals despite limited resources.

Call to Action

◊ Learn from the experiences of successful individuals such as Capt. Sully who achieved success in 40 years, and the businesswoman who accomplished it in 19 years. Understand that their achievements materialize over time.

◊ Remain calm, think critically, and always act with precision, even when it is a split-second decision when faced with complex challenges or situations.

◊ Embrace the opportunities that come your way, even if they require you to invest time and resources.

◊ Do not be discouraged by setbacks or failures; learn from them and keep pushing forward to achieve your dreams. Focus on the things you can control.

◊ Prioritize personal growth and development by learning new skills and acquiring knowledge via online platforms like Coursera.

◊ Network with others, both online and offline, yet to give value to others rather than for selfish reasons.

◊ Be resourceful by finding creative solutions to problems and leveraging available resources.

- CHAPTER FIVE -

Stooping to Conquer

"For those who exalt themselves will be humbled, and those who humble themselves will be exalted."

Matthew 23:12

In 2015, I took on the task of organizing a conference centered around the theme of "Passion to Profit." At that time, there was a growing interest among women to learn how to transform their passions into a sustainable source of income. Coming from a predominantly patriarchal society, I understand firsthand the challenges that women face when relying on others for their daily needs.
In 2015, I took on the task of organizing a conference centered around the theme of "Passion to Profit." At that time, there was a growing interest among women to learn how to transform their passions into a sustainable source of income. Coming from a predominantly patriarchal society, I

understand firsthand the challenges women face when relying on others for their daily needs.

My goal with the conference was to empower women and provide them with the tools and knowledge they need to turn their passions into profitable businesses. Regardless of a woman's background, education, age, or social status, every woman has unique and remarkable talents that can be put to practical use to attain financial independence. Women can achieve economic autonomy and create a fulfilling and successful careers with the right mindset and resources.

The conference had a profound impact, attracting many women eager to join the movement. With the resounding success and to keep the momentum going, I established my inner circle network, now known as the Seun Akinlotan Network (SAN).

Since its inception, SAN has undergone a transformational journey, evolving into a robust platform for personal growth and leadership development. Our network is driven by a vision to empower members to unleash their full potential and live fulfilling lives. Through our community, we aim to create a supportive environment that fosters growth, collaboration, and positive change.

The birth of SAN resulted from the success of the "Passion to Profit" conference, which sparked a desire to create a lasting impact on women's lives. Our network has become a space where women can come together, share experiences, and learn from one another to reach their full potential.

In a recent weekly session at our network, we delved into the story of Joseph from the Bible. We examined its practical applications in everyday life. Joseph was born into a polygamous family, and his father showed him particular favoritism by gifting him a coat of many colors, which brought him great joy. Unfortunately, this act of affection incited jealousy in his siblings.

As if the display of his father's love wasn't enough, Joseph compounded the issue by sharing a dream in which his siblings and parents would bow down to him.

Joseph eagerly began to share his dream with his siblings, saying, "Listen to this dream that I have had: As we were binding sheaves in the field, my sheaf rose and stood upright, while your sheaves gathered around mine and bowed down to it." However, he was unaware that sharing his dream would only exacerbate his brothers' envy and alienate them further.

As time passed, Joseph's brothers became consumed with jealousy. They hoped to crush his dreams of dominating their family entirely. When the opportunity arose, they conspired to sell him into slavery.

Amazingly, he remained remarkably composed and unruffled throughout the ordeal, as depicted in biblical accounts. Despite being sold into slavery and facing numerous challenges, Joseph maintained a calm and graceful demeanor, choosing to focus on his work and producing exceptional results in everything he did.

Upon arriving in Egypt, Joseph secured employment with one of the country's most prominent officials, Potiphar. During his time in Potiphar's service, it became apparent that Joseph brought good fortune to the household, prompting Potiphar to promote him to the position of the household head. Despite being a foreigner in a strange land, Joseph's access to all of Potiphar's resources emphasizes the significance of diligence over one's location.

Before long, in a bizarre twist of events, Joseph found himself in captivity after Potiphar's wife falsely accused him of attempted rape. Despite this unjust imprisonment, Joseph remained focused on his duties and continued to carry out his responsibilities faithfully. Joseph's dedication and hard work did not go unnoticed, as the prison warden eventually promoted him to captain.

Joseph possessed a remarkable quality that I deeply admire: his ability to demonstrate leadership qualities in any situation. Joseph could remain optimistic and maintain his high spirits if things were not going according to plan or if he faced false accusations.

Even in prison, Joseph's leadership qualities shone through when he assisted his fellow inmates in interpreting their dreams. One of those prisoners was the butler of Pharaoh, whom Joseph interpreted as his dream, predicting his eventual release and restoration to his former position. Joseph asked the butler not to forget him once he was released. Still, unfortunately, the butler forgot about him for two years. Despite this setback, Joseph remained content and did not allow bitterness to consume him. He continued to hold onto hope and maintained a positive outlook.

Joseph remained composed when the butler finally remembered him and recommended him to Pharoah as a potential dream interpreter. Ultimately, he was appointed as Egypt's prime minister, and he had a fateful encounter with his brothers, who had earlier sold him into slavery. Irrespective of their previous actions, Joseph chose not to seek revenge on them. Instead, he humbly interacted with them, to the point that they unknowingly bowed before him. This display of grace and forgiveness is an exemplary trait that we can all learn from.

Yes, Joseph's journey was filled with curveballs — unexpected twists and turns — thrown at him. Still, his ability to remain focused and productive in adversity is a testament to his resilience and inner strength. Despite his circumstances, he refused to succumb to bitterness or despair. Instead, he chose to make the most of his situation. His approach serves as a powerful example of what it means to "stoop and conquer."

By maintaining a positive mindset, focusing on his goals, and humbling himself, he overcame even the most daunting obstacles and achieved greatness.

What is your response when faced with unfavorable odds? Do you crumble under pressure? How do you handle it when it appears as though the promises of God for your life are not being fulfilled? Please take a few moments to reflect on these questions.

Building Capacity

I have a great passion for event planning, and it has been a favorite task of mine since childhood. My first official event planning gig was for my 10th birthday party, where I had a clear vision for the location, guests, food, and even music. While the music aspect did not turn out as I envisioned, the event was still a huge success. Even adults were impressed that a young child like me could handle event planning.

As I grew older and attended more events, my passion for planning events grew stronger. So, many years ago, when I started brainstorming potential business ideas, event planning was at the top of my list.

I initially aimed to plan weddings and other special events from beginning to end. However, despite trying to understand the market, the business grew slower than I had hoped. Then, one day, a seasoned event planner gave me an incredible chance to shadow her as she planned a wedding for a client. She took me through the whole process, and I observed how she managed the groom's and bride's families and all the vendors involved.

After observing the veteran event planner, I was impressed by the enormous energy, coordination, and effort required to execute an event of such magnitude flawlessly. It became clear that although I possessed the skills to plan a wedding, I still needed to develop my capacity to ensure that I could deliver exceptional service to my clients. Shadowing an experienced professional made me realize I had a long road before confidently taking on the events I had always dreamed of planning.

What actions did I take next? Following that realization, I firmly committed to seeking guidance from more experienced event planners who better understood the industry's community, landscape, and nuances.

Are you adequately prepared to achieve your dreams? I am grateful that I realized the importance of building capacity as an event planner before I landed my dream gig.

While having passion is crucial, it alone is not sufficient. Capacity building is critical to success, especially when facing significant challenges. Even if you invest time and effort in building capacity for a particular project or task, it may yield little results. I suggest that you persevere. By persevering with a determined spirit, you can stay focused and motivated. The great news is that when the opportunity finally arises, you will be well-prepared to seize it, and your efforts will be recognized.

In Chapter 4, I cited the examples of David and Capt. Sully, who both prepared for opportunities long before they arose. David was a shepherd boy who tended to his father's flock in the wilderness while his brothers served in the Israeli army. He cared for, nurtured, and protected the community from predators as a shepherd. During this time, he trained himself to tactically defeat dangerous predators such as lions and bears with his bare hands. This was no easy feat, and one can only imagine the effort he must have put into building his muscular and tactical abilities to handle such powerful animals.

David's capacity-building efforts were eventually put to use when the need arose. Goliath, a giant from a neighboring country, had been threatening the Israelites incessantly, and many warriors in the Israeli army were intimidated by his imposing physical presence. When David heard of Goliath's threats, he fearlessly stepped forward. He successfully brought down the giant with a single stone from his slingshot, much to the amazement of the entire nation.

Predictably, news of David's victory over Goliath quickly spread, and crowds flocked to praise him for his bravery and determination. While this was a significant moment for the nation, many failed to realize that David's triumph was not a stroke of luck.

Before confronting Goliath, David had shared with Saul, the King of Israel then, that he was ready for the task. He recounted how he had previously fought off both a bear and a lion with his bare hands while caring for his father's sheep. David's ability to successfully fight off such fierce animals with his bare hands served as the foundation upon which he built his capacity as a fighter. As a result, when the situation demanded it, David could deliver an entire nation from oppression, terror, and the threat of destruction.

Building capacity for your skills is essential to achieve success in life and overcoming challenges. This means developing your abilities and knowledge, even when there may not be immediate opportunities available to apply them. David's story is a prime example of how building capacity can lead to victory.

What should you do when there are no opportunities available? It's easy to become discouraged and give up, but focusing on building your capacity for a needed skill is vital. This means taking the time to learn, practice and develop your abilities, even if there are no immediate opportunities to apply them. When the opportunity eventually arises, you will be ready to seize it and excel.

Applying the 10,000-Hour Rule

As someone passionate about event planning, I am filled with joy and curiosity whenever I attend meticulously planned events. During summertime, several churches in my area host weeklong events for children, and I decided many years ago to enroll my daughter in one of these summer kids' clubs. Although my main goal was for her to enjoy the activities and make new friends, I had no high expectations beyond that. However, by the end of the week, I was astonished by the exceptional organization and precision of planning the event and the remarkable outcomes.

I decided to volunteer for the church event in July of that year. However, I wondered, "How did the church organize such an impressive event?" Since I had no connections with the church community then, I felt awkward about asking the organizers directly. Instead, I opted to observe the event closely for an extended period. It wasn't until the event's last day that they made an announcement calling for volunteers.

The following week, I received an email outlining the plans for the upcoming year, including weekly meetings from September to June. At our first meeting, we had over 100 volunteers in attendance, and the discussion, planning, and collaboration made it feel like the event was just a few days away. As an event planning enthusiast, I was grateful to witness how investing time in planning even a small event for children could make it turn out flawlessly.

Achieving greatness or excellence often requires dedication and investment of time, money, and resources. Being part of the planning process for the kids' event opened my eyes to the importance of giving my best effort in everything I do, regardless of whether it may receive recognition.

In his book "Outliers: The Story of Success," Malcolm Gladwell emphasized that "practice is not the thing you do once you are good. It is the thing you do that makes you good." Gladwell discussed "The 10,000-Hour Rule" and how it was crucial to the Beatles' success. The band had the chance to perform live as a group in Hamburg, Germany, over 1,200 times between 1960 and 1964, which helped them hone their musical skills and become world-famous musicians.

Whether or not you agree with Gladwell's theory, It is crucial to prioritize investing quality time to achieve excellence. A successful event is not a stroke of luck; it demands meticulous planning and practice sessions behind the scenes. Organizers must stay awake when others are asleep because many hours must be devoted to perfecting a 120-minute event. Whenever I attended the church's event, it seemed almost surreal to most people, and only those involved in the background understood the immense amount of time and resources invested in planning it.

To truly excel, you must be willing to go above and beyond what is expected and put in the necessary work to achieve greatness. Achieving success and standing out from the rest requires a willingness to invest time and effort in perfecting your skills, even against the odds. It may also require working with other professionals, but leadership and direction are crucial to help the team excel.

Serve Before You Deserve

During one of my visits to Abeokuta, my hometown, I had the opportunity to explore Olumo Rock, a popular tourist attraction. Accompanied by some companions, we were greeted by an unofficial tour guide upon arrival. To my surprise, I discovered that this young man was speech impaired.

As the tour drew to a close, the attitude of our speech-impaired guide revealed a fundamental principle of overcoming obstacles that elude many. Despite his inability to communicate verbally, he employed his cheerful disposition and made the most of what he had. He refused to let his situation dampen his spirits, and his mastery of every nook and cranny of the site was impressive. He even offered to lead us through seemingly treacherous terrains, quickly navigating them and using precise gestures to indicate the way. His infectious excitement stood out most, which made us feel like we had hit the jackpot.

After our tour, we were filled with a sense of achievement and satisfaction. There is a profound feeling of indescribable joy that comes from accomplishing something that you once thought was impossible. Our speech-impaired guide exceeded our expectations, leaving us thoroughly impressed with his remarkable abilities and exceptional service. For the stated reasons, we unanimously agreed to pay him more than his standard fee as a token of our appreciation.

And that's not all. To commemorate our unforgettable experience, we took turns taking pictures with him, captivated by his infectious positivity and unwavering dedication to his craft. It was evident that he had a deep passion for his work, and his unparalleled service left an indelible impression on us. His attitude and commitment to serving his clients evoked blessings. They reinforced a guiding principle everyone should live by–serve before you deserve.

Volunteering is a Tool for Greatness

Oyinkansola (Ayobiojo) Bayode currently serves as the Vice President of a Fortune-500 investment management firm in Boston, Massachusetts. Despite experiencing the devastating loss of her father at the tender age of five, Oyinkansola had an enriching childhood. Growing up in a single-parent household taught Oyinkansola invaluable life skills. It forced her to mature at a young age. Following her father's passing, she, her mother, and two brothers relocated to Boston to start anew.

At just six years old, Oyinkansola began helping with household chores, taking on a more significant role in the family's day-to-day life. She witnessed her mother's unwavering work ethic and resilience as she worked tirelessly to provide for her children and rebuild their lives from scratch. These experiences taught Oyinkansola the importance of hard work, determination, and perseverance in adversity. These lessons would serve her well throughout her life, contributing to her success as a prominent figure in investment management.

"I vividly remember moving into our first apartment, and the four of us slept on the mattress in the living room the first night. We did not have much, but we were so happy to have our place," she narrated.

Oyinkansola had a clear vision of her future career path after attending a three-week business camp called the "LEAD Program in Business" during the summer after her junior year. The program at the University of Georgia introduced her to various aspects of the business world, including finance, accounting, marketing, and more. The program also included company visits and a case competition.

During this program, she discovered her passion for business and wrote her first business plan at 16. Her talents were quickly recognized, and her team won second place in the case competition. This experience further fueled her passion for business and solidified her desire to pursue a career in the field. From a young age, it was clear that Oyinkansola possessed a natural talent for entrepreneurship and had the drive and determination necessary to succeed in the business world.

When Oyin graduated from high school, she was among the top 10% of her class. She secured full scholarships to Harvard University and The Wharton School at the University of Pennsylvania. Ultimately, she opted to attend the University of Pennsylvania, where she graduated with honors, debt-free. Her college internship at Goldman Sachs sustained her interest in finance and has earned her bachelor's degree. She enrolled in a Master's in Business Administration at New York University (NYU) in 2016.

In the fall semester of 2016, Oyinkansola embarked on a mission to secure an internship in investment banking for the following summer. This involved attending an overwhelming number of corporate presentations and informational meetings every week and managing her coursework. Despite the rigorous schedule, she recognized the value of networking and was determined to do whatever it took to succeed.

In October 2016, an opportunity presented itself when she was asked to volunteer at a conference focused on private equity for women. Although attending the conference as a student was no longer financially feasible, she knew the event planner. She was offered a trip to Chicago along with additional support. At the conference, she had the chance to meet a managing director from an investment bank in New York City. She remained in contact with her for several months.

Three months of navigating the structured on-campus recruitment process ended, and Oyinkansola had interviewed with eight banks, completing 20 rounds of interviews.

Unfortunately, she did not secure an offer, and by February 2017, she felt ashamed and disappointed. However, she refused to give up and instead contacted her contacts, including the managing director she had met at the conference. The director offered her another opportunity to interview. After much prayer and preparation, she finally received an offer for the internship. Her hard work and persistence paid off, and she was able to thrive during the summer internship.

It is no surprise that Oyinkansola has achieved success in her career, as she is one of the few people I know who is truly dedicated to service and hard work. When she commits to something, she gives it her all, and the tangible results speak for themselves. I remember organizing a "Beyond Ordinary" event in Philadelphia in 2016. Oyinkansola was one of the volunteers who stepped up to help. She attended every meeting with dedication, offered invaluable ideas that significantly impacted the outcome, and even acted as the event's emcee. It's inspiring to see her continue to grow and achieve great things, all thanks to her deep understanding of the value of serving and volunteering. It has provided a solid foundation for her to reach new heights in life.

> "What if I do not have access to opportunities for volunteering?" a lady once asked me during a roundtable session.

You may be in the same shoes where your community needs more volunteer opportunities. If so, consider creating one in your environment to make a difference or looking for them online. Also, try to avoid seeing the act of volunteering as something you have to do in organizations known to solicit volunteers. It could be something as simple as cleaning up your neighborhood, teaching children about godly virtues, or working on a project that will benefit other people outside of your immediate family members.

Volunteering is a selfless act that can positively impact both the giver and the receiver. When you volunteer, you are helping others and opening yourself up to new opportunities. Volunteering can provide a sense of purpose and fulfillment, leading to personal growth and development. It can also help you develop new skills, make new connections, and gain valuable experience that can be useful in your personal and professional life.

If you want to overcome challenges and achieve success in life, it's essential to be willing to give back to others. Whether donating money, volunteering your time, or using your skills and resources to help others, giving can transform your life. By focusing on the needs of others, you can gain a new perspective on your challenges and develop empathy and compassion that can help you in all areas of your life.

Finding causes that align with your values and passions is essential to maximize the benefits of volunteering. This will help you stay motivated and engaged in the work, making it more likely that you will continue to volunteer and reap the rewards of the experience. Remember, volunteering is not just about doing good for others; it's also about doing good for yourself. By giving of yourself, you can create a better world for all and find success in your own life.

Call to Action

◊ Become independent by putting your talents to practical use, especially if you are a woman.

◊ Learn from the story of Joseph: when faced with adversity in life, maintain a positive attitude.

◊ Developing your capacity is crucial for both personal and professional success. It would help if you went above and beyond as a leader by constantly enhancing your abilities. By offering exceptional guidance, you can inspire your team to achieve greatness.

◊ Set apart quality time, and invest money and resources to achieve excellence in anything you do.

◊ Use volunteering as a tool for networking opportunities.

◊ Take advantage of opportunities and programs that align with your interests to solidify your career path.

◊ Learn to stoop to conquer, and refrain from bitterness and vindictiveness.

- CHAPTER SIX -

Overcoming Roadblocks

"We will either find a way or make one."

Hannibal

During my first year in college, I faced challenges that tested my faith in many ways. Firstly, I enrolled in a college I only knew about a few months before my admission. My original ambition was to become a medical doctor since I had always excelled in the sciences. As a child, I was constantly told I would one day become a doctor. However, when my first two attempts to pursue this path proved unsuccessful, my parents introduced me to the University of Agriculture in my hometown.

Having no prior knowledge of the college's existence, I initially thought it was a prank. After all, my childhood dream was to attend a medical college outside of Rock City. Doing so would have provided an opportunity to explore new horizons. However, my parents insisted, and I eventually gave in to visiting the campus for a tour. Realizing that the college existed left me feeling overwhelmed, but my parents tried to alleviate my disappointment.

At that time, the school had both mini and main campuses, and considering the ease of access to each location, I decided to visit the mini campus first. As I strolled through the campus, I couldn't help but notice how much it resembled a church rather than a college. Not only that, after perusing the brochure, none of the courses offered aligned with my plans for a future career. Many students at the time typically chose to study agricultural economics, a course that was not an option for me. And to make matters worse, I was conflicted about the school's proximity to home. I felt trounced.

My parents suggested that attending a school that didn't align with my initial preference was preferable to remaining idle at home for another year. They encouraged me by saying that once I was enrolled in a school, I could reapply to study medicine at a federal school within the region. Following a few weeks of self-denial, I eventually came to terms with the situation and accepted that I had no other option but to attend the University of Agriculture.

After extensive research, I ultimately chose to study environmental management and toxicology (EMT). My parents were hesitant about my decision, as the environmental industry in Nigeria was still in its early stages. However, I assured them that I had carefully considered the potential career opportunities and was making an informed choice. Regardless of my field of study, my ability to contribute and create value in any organization would determine my career advancement.

The beginning of my college journey was marked by a prolonged period of despair as I struggled to come to terms with my new reality. Without a clear plan or strategy to cope with my situation, I felt like the weight of the world was crashing down on me, and no one seemed to understand the depth of my pain. I confided in one of my friends, expressing my frustration and repeating repeatedly, "This is not where I am supposed to be." However, her response was less than empathetic, urging me to stop crying over spilled milk.

As time passed, the first semester of college passed in a blur, and before I knew it, it was time for exams. Although I performed well, I couldn't help but feel that I could have done better if I had focused and studied harder. Nonetheless, my performance gave me a glimmer of hope and reassurance that I could overcome the challenges ahead.

The second-semester classes, however, posed more significant challenges that demanded even more commitment from me. Despite my increased efforts, I struggled to maintain focus and keep up with my readings. When the results were released, it was evident that I had dropped the ball in one of my courses, organic chemistry. Scoring below the pass mark significantly affected my record of never having failed a course or class. The realization left me feeling devastated.

Soon enough, it was the start of the second year. Reflecting on the semester break, I realized that my post-graduation success depends entirely on my character rather than external factors.

I also realized that my friend was correct; lamenting about the past would not aid me in achieving my desired future. I understood that if I persisted with such an attitude, I might end up failing more courses, prolonging my stay in school, and having an unsatisfactory academic record. Therefore, I consciously decided to give my all to my studies. Even though studying environmental management and toxicology was not my initial career choice, there was still a high potential to create a fulfilling future.

Reflecting on my past, I can now appreciate the twists and turns of my journey. Although I initially struggled to make sense of the situation, I persevered and succeeded despite the adversity. Despite the disappointment of not being accepted into medical school, attending the University of Agriculture provided me with valuable life skills that I have been able to apply whenever I encounter obstacles on my path.

Through my experiences at the University of Agriculture, I learned the importance of resilience and adaptability. I realized that life rarely goes according to plan and that the ability to pivot and adjust to changing circumstances is essential for success. Additionally, I learned to embrace new opportunities and experiences, even if they were not what I had initially envisioned for myself.

As I faced the challenges of adjusting to a new school and pursuing a different field of study, I also learned the importance of self-reflection and self-improvement. I recognized the need to prioritize my goals and focus on the most important things to me. I achieved academic success through dedication and hard work and built a foundation for my future.

Overall, I am grateful for the obstacles I faced and the lessons I learned at the University of Agriculture. These experiences have equipped me with the skills and mindset necessary to overcome roadblocks and pursue my goals, no matter how difficult the journey is.

Accelerating Your Growth

Dr. Oluwaseun Ogunjimi, whom I affectionately call Dr. Seun, is not only my friend but also a senior director at a prestigious university in the United States. Our paths crossed nearly two decades ago when we were both searching for direction in life. Before assuming her current role, Dr. Seun worked at a health analytics firm, where she dutifully reported to work every weekday.

At that time, she had a demanding morning routine that involved dropping off her two toddlers at daycare before embarking on a 55-mile commute to work, which she did every weekday to arrive before 8 a.m. Her afternoon routine followed the same pattern but in reverse.

Her ability to juggle her responsibilities always amazed me, so I often asked her, "How can you pull this off?" She would respond, "I might not be able to tell you how I pulled it off, but I find myself pulling it off somehow."

She continued this routine for two years until one day when she arrived at work and was informed by her boss that the recession had affected the company. As a result, they had to make difficult decisions, including letting go of some employees.

It felt surreal when she informed me that she had lost her job. I couldn't fathom how such a hardworking and dedicated professional could be let go. However, as the days went by, the harsh reality began to sink in, and I knew it was time for her to chart a new course. One day, my phone rang, and it was her. I answered eagerly, hoping to hear about a new job prospect.

I was taken aback when Dr. Seun told me she had decided to return to school to pursue a completely different career, abandoning years of hard work and notable achievements as a chartered accountant. Although I was concerned about how she would manage a growing family, I also knew she was a determined achiever who would never settle for less, no matter the challenges.

Dr. Seun was determined to make her new career aspirations come true. Despite having a growing family and financial constraints, she took evening classes for two years while working part-time with little income. Throughout this period, she embodied the virtue of prioritizing her long-term goal over her present unpleasant circumstances. Though bills needed to be paid, she understood that taking shortcuts or sacrificing her career growth would not bring her the future she desired. This meant cutting back significantly on socializing outside of family and close friends, but it was a sacrifice she was willing to make for her future success.

After completing her evening classes, Dr. Seun excelled in all the prerequisite courses required for admission into Nursing School. She earned a Bachelor of Science, a Master of Science in Nursing, and a Doctor of Nursing degree, a remarkable accomplishment that can only be achieved by those with a solid drive to succeed.

During one of our conversations, she shared a passage from Proverbs 24:27 that continues to inspire her. The verse emphasizes the importance of counting costs and planning before starting a new venture. She uses this verse as a guiding principle to determine what needs to be done, the resources required, and the steps necessary to achieve her goals.

Despite her impressive academic achievements, Dr. Seun encountered several challenges. One of the significant challenges she faced was the issue of reduced income. She had to adjust her lifestyle significantly and reduce expenses to cope with the reduced income while pursuing her studies. In addition, she had to deal with the issue of being in class with much younger coursemates who had just graduated from high school. It was challenging for her to connect with them and integrate with the group. Communication with professors and other people was also a significant challenge she had to navigate, given the cultural and language differences that existed.

Furthermore, Dr. Seun had to learn to take tests and pass with flying colors. This was incredibly challenging because she was pursuing a new career path and had to learn new skills and concepts. Despite all these challenges, she persevered and worked hard to achieve her goals.

Today, Dr. Seun is one of the happiest people around and loves her job. She finds it fulfilling and wakes up eager to go to work every morning. She accelerated her career growth significantly in the last decade because she gave it her all. The lesson from her journey is that accelerating one's growth and achieving success requires hard work, determination, and a willingness to push through challenges.

Keeping Things in Perspective

John Eckart* was an accomplished builder known for his precision, attention to detail, and ability to craft exceptional works of art. He worked at one of the most prestigious construction firms in the world, where he built a reputation as a master builder. However, in the final ten years of his career, the atmosphere at his company began to shift. The year-on-year financial forecasts for the organization began to decline, forcing senior management to implement across-the-board cuts.

Despite the company's decision to make across-the-board cuts, John was fortunate to have earned great respect and admiration from his colleagues due to his invaluable contributions to the company's growth. As a result, instead of being let go and potentially jeopardizing his prospects for a good retirement life, the company decided to reduce his wages by 10%. While initially infuriated by the decision, he ultimately decided to stay on board with the company.

With a reduced income, John's work ethic deteriorated, and he exhibited a lackadaisical attitude toward his job. He became increasingly tardy, missed deadlines, and produced substandard work. As a result, customers and managers began to voice their dissatisfaction with the buildings he was in charge of. Despite his underperformance, the company still kept him on board.

Eventually, after 30 years of service, John announced his decision to resign. The news of his departure spread quickly, and the managers agreed to request that he construct one last house before leaving the company.

"Please build one more house before you quit," they pleaded with him.

John approached the task with a fixed mindset, doing the bare minimum and producing subpar work. On his last day, the company held a retirement party in his honor, which was well-attended by both old and new employees. During a speech by the top manager, John was called to the center of the venue to receive his parting gift.

"John, after 30 years of meritorious service, all the managers met and decided that you deserve a special gift," he began to express to the reverberating applause of the attendees. "The last house we pleaded with you to build was for you, and here are the keys. Please do enjoy your retirement," the top manager concluded.

John was surprised, and the realization that he had brought the situation upon himself brought tears of despair to his eyes. The day to celebrate his career had turned into a nightmare. If he had only seen things from a different perspective, he could have gone home with the keys to his dream home. Unfortunately, his inability to adapt to the 10% wage cut during the recession forced him to experience what he had inflicted on others.

In contrast, let me share a heartwarming story I read on Instagram about a woman named Rose (not her real name). Rose is an event decorator known for her exceptional skills and creative ideas that set her work apart. Recently, she got engaged to the man of her dreams, and her fiancé decided it was time to make their engagement public. He organized a surprise announcement and enlisted the help of a few trusted friends to plan the event. The planners then devised a brilliant idea to trick Rose into decorating the venue for the announcement, where her fiancé would propose to her.

Despite being unaware of the event's real purpose, Rose went above and beyond to decorate the venue, ensuring that every detail was perfect. She was even informed that she would only receive payment after the event, yet she did not skimp on her work. Finally, the day of the announcement arrived, and Rose was stunned to discover that it was her fiancé proposing to her. Her hard work and dedication had set the perfect stage for the love of her life to pop the question, and the surprise announcement turned into a beautiful engagement.

Overcoming Roadblocks

This story is a testament to the importance of hard work, dedication, and going above and beyond in every task we undertake. It also shows how small acts of kindness and thoughtfulness can significantly impact someone's life. Despite the uncertainty of payment, Rose's commitment to her work paid off in a big way and resulted in a perfect proposal from the man of her dreams. The planners and Rose's fiancé's efforts to surprise her with a proposal in a beautifully decorated venue made it a day she will never forget.

How do you handle life issues that do not align with your expectations? Do you keep things in perspective even when the future looks bleak? Do you withdraw and cease giving your best or stay diligent regardless of the prevailing challenges?

Life is full of ups and downs, and often things do not go according to plan. When faced with unexpected challenges, it can be easy to become discouraged, lose sight of your goals, and start slacking on your responsibilities. However, keeping things in perspective and maintaining a positive attitude is essential.

Reframing your thinking is one way to handle issues outside of your expectations. Instead of focusing on the negative aspects of the situation, you can choose to see the positive and look for opportunities to learn and grow. This shift in perspective can help you stay motivated and focused on your goals, even in difficult times.

Another critical factor in handling unexpected challenges is diligence. It can be tempting to withdraw and give up when things do not go your way, but this will only lead to further disappointment. Instead, you should continue to work hard and give your best effort, even when faced with obstacles. This determination and perseverance will help you overcome adversity and achieve your goals.

Ultimately, putting things in perspective is crucial for navigating life's challenges. By reframing your thinking, maintaining a positive attitude, and staying diligent, you can overcome the most difficult obstacles and succeed.

Utilizing the Power of Positive Associations

Mayowa Ekundayo's story resonates with many people worldwide. Despite growing up in a challenging environment that would have broken the self-esteem of many children, he persevered and overcame his complicated past. His story was so compelling that it needed to be shared with more people, and I am honored to retell it here.

Mayowa is a Nigerian who grew up in a home where he witnessed things that no child should ever have to experience. His father, a military man, was often verbally abusive and used physical violence to intimidate and control his family.

> "I saw a lot of things that children should not have experienced. I witnessed verbal abuse, threats, and physical violence from my father, a military man," he shared during an interview.

He began working at 14 due to his family's financial struggles. Working as a bus conductor alongside his father in Lagos State, Nigeria, he often worked for about three hours before going to school. Their route was the same as the one that led to Mr. Ekundayo's school, increasing the likelihood that some of his schoolmates would board the bus.

"I typically hid my face so no one would recognize me," he said.

He described how his experience as a bus conductor led him to develop a sense of low self-worth and unconsciously adopt a "failure" mindset. This negative mindset had such a profound impact on him that by the time he gained college admission, he would frequently tell his friends to remember him when they eventually succeeded. Thankfully, his friends consistently encouraged him by reminding him of his potential and that he could achieve anything he set his mind to rather than surrendering to his fate. With the support of his friends, he gradually overcame the "failure" mindset.

Today, Mayowa is an entrepreneur taking giant strides in his community as an infopreneur and living a fulfilled life against all odds. He credited his ability to rise above the failure mindset to his friends for their boldness in challenging him not to settle for less while influencing him positively.

Positive associations can significantly influence an individual's life, particularly in achieving success and overcoming challenges. According to research, an individual tends to become like the people he is consistently associated with, which highlights the importance of choosing the right company to keep. Surrounding oneself with great, like-minded individuals who share the same values and aspirations can profoundly impact one's life.

When you surround yourself with motivated, ambitious individuals focused on achieving their goals, you are likelier to adopt these positive traits and develop similar characteristics. Such people will inspire you to strive for greatness, push your limits, and hold you accountable for your actions.

On the other hand, surrounding yourself with people who are always complaining and dwelling on their problems can harm your life. These individuals can drag you down, fill your mind with negative thoughts, and discourage you from pursuing your dreams.

Therefore, you must surround yourself with positive influences that can push you toward success and personal growth. Choosing the right company can be a game-changer in life, and it is up to you to make the necessary changes and seek out the right people who can support and guide you toward your goals.

Call to Action

◊ Cultivate a positive mindset about detours, and rather than seeing them as roadblocks, view them as opportunities to learn and grow and to explore new paths that you may not have considered before.

◊ Maintain a positive outlook, stay motivated, and develop uncommon resilience in adversity.

◊ Reflect and develop a sound strategy for moving forward in an unpleasant situation.

◊ Keep things in perspective when dealing with issues in life, and do not let a negative mindset or experience overshadow your potential for success.

◊ Keep adding value to yourself irrespective of your course of study or career path, the workplace, or the organization.

◊ Show up and do your best regardless of the situation and circumstances.

- CHAPTER SEVEN -

Stirring the Stagnant Waters

"The will to win, the desire to succeed, the urge to reach your full potential; these are the keys that will unlock the door to personal excellence."

Confucius

Have you ever observed that whenever you step into a new environment, those who arrived before you seem to follow certain rules? These rules could apply to a variety of settings, such as a school, church, workplace, or even a country. These experienced individuals possess knowledge of the intricacies of the location and can advise on what will or will not function.

Have you ever observed that those who arrived before you followed specific rules whenever you entered a new environment? These experienced individuals possess knowledge of the intricacies of the location and can advise on what will or will not function. Also, these rules could apply to various settings, such as a school, church, workplace, or country.

During my undergraduate years, I was required to complete a capstone project. In anticipation of this, I interviewed several students who had previously completed the project, but many focused on subjects divergent from my areas of interest.

However, one day, I unexpectedly had the opportunity to participate in a research expedition with some scientists to conduct a sample survey. Although I wasn't supposed to be in the group, I was in the right place and time.

When we reached the sampling site, we were taken aback by the extent of water quality degradation resulting from untreated industrial effluent that had entered an unnamed tributary of a major river. As we observed several dead fish, I was utterly dismayed that no one else seemed to share my concern.

> "There is nothing we can do about it," one of the senior colleagues told me then, but the situation bothered me greatly.

The body of water served as a source of livelihood for the people whose main occupation was fishing. Beyond that, I was concerned about the far-reaching implications for aquatic life, the food the people consumed and their health. That was when I conceived the idea for my final-year project as an undergraduate. I wanted to explore "The Effects of Industrial Effluents on Aquatic Life."

After gradually progressing, I reached my fifth and final year of undergraduate studies. This year was the most memorable as I was fully engaged in schoolwork. Not only had I grown physically, but I had also developed in my thoughts, words, and actions. I had let go of my excuses, felt a greater responsibility and was ready to tackle any academic challenge.

Because of my experience witnessing water quality degradation, I clearly understood what I wanted to research, the time required to conduct the research, and the necessary tools and resources. Soon enough, it was time to submit the topic for my capstone project to my assigned supervisor. During our initial group meeting, my supervisor remarked,

> "You possess remarkable clarity." After receiving his approval, I immediately dove into the project.

My project required me to work in the laboratory with live fish purchased from a fish field. The cost of the fish was quite expensive, and I found myself tempted to reduce the amount needed to save money. However, to achieve the desired results, I needed to simulate the natural habitat of the fish in the laboratory while introducing varying concentrations of effluent, such as paint and detergent, to measure the time it would take for half of the fish to die in effluent-saturated concentrations.

Conducting this experiment required a significant amount of time throughout the project. In addition, I had to balance my other obligations as a student, including completing my required courses.

Several months into the project, my supervisor called me and the other students under his supervision to his office to deliver some surprising news. He announced that he had accepted an offer at another school. As I attempted to process this information and consider its impact on the continuity of our projects, one of my fellow students asked,

> "Will you still be our supervisor?"

The room fell silent as everyone waited for his response, their eyes fixed on him in anticipation.

> "Unfortunately, I will not be able to continue as your supervisor as I will be preoccupied with my new role once I start there," he responded somberly.

Eventually, I was assigned a new supervisor. However, to my dismay, she claimed she knew nothing about my project and asked me to submit a new topic and start over.

At first, I thought she was making a joke, but as she repeated her request, it became apparent that she was serious. I sought further clarification, hoping for leniency, but she remained resolute that I must begin from scratch. Given my progress and the substantial amount of money I had invested, I had to make a compelling case to persuade her to let me proceed with my current project. As a result, unlike the other students assigned new supervisors and had to research entirely new topics, I was favored to continue with my existing project.

> "What would have happened if I refused to plead for leniency?" I frequently asked myself.

Refusing to do so would have resulted in a waste of my money, time, and resources. As a student, I could not afford to be careless with my finances. Even if I had unlimited funds, every penny was valuable to me, and the time that had already passed was irretrievable.

The incident taught me the importance of persevering through obstacles and stirring the waters to uncover what lies beneath the surface. Rather than simply accepting a setback, it is crucial to explore every avenue and not give up easily.

One of my favorite Bible verses, found in Matthew 7:7, speaks to this idea:

> "Ask and it will be given to you; seek and you will find; knock and the door will be opened to you."

By following these principles, I have achieved many great things in life. Of course, there have been times when my efforts were not immediately rewarded, but I have found peace knowing that I acted in good faith and did not give up.

Stirring the stagnant waters is a concept that involves taking action to change the current state of things to uncover hidden opportunities or solutions. It is a powerful tool for anyone who desires success in their personal and professional life. However, some people may need to be more familiar with this concept or apply it more. If you are in this category, it is time to take action and apply this concept.

When you take action to stir the stagnant waters, you become more proactive and intentional about the results you are getting in your life. You take control of your circumstances and rely less on external factors to determine your success. This sense of power can be empowering and help you achieve your goals faster.

Stirring the stagnant waters will uncover hidden opportunities and solutions you would not have otherwise discovered. Stirring the stagnant waters can also lead to breakthroughs in your personal and professional life and can help you to achieve success more quickly.

It is time to start if you still need to apply the concept of stirring stagnant waters. By doing so, you will take control of your life, become more intentional about the results you are getting, and uncover hidden opportunities and solutions that can help you to achieve success.

Understanding the Power of Persistence

One of my enduring aspirations is to empower people. It gives me great satisfaction to collaborate with those who have felt that the life they aspire to is unattainable and to help them transform their aspirations into tangible achievements.

Achieving my goal of empowering others took a lot of work. I started at a young age, teaching subjects like mathematics, integrated science, and social studies to those who struggled with them. Additionally, I enjoyed sharing Bible stories with children who did not have access to them. In college, I regularly hosted friends for study sessions at my place, and it was rewarding to see them excel academically with my help. I felt humbled and grateful for the opportunity to impact their lives positively. Witnessing their joy and sense of liberation after achieving academic success reinforced my desire to continue empowering others. Although I did not know how then, I believed that God was preparing me for more extraordinary things in the future.

After relocating to the United States, I faced a steep learning curve in understanding how the system worked. Determined to succeed, I took the initiative to learn as much as possible about the country and its workings. To achieve this, I invested in my personal development by attending conferences and training sessions and reading books by renowned authors and leadership experts such as John Maxwell, Brian Tracy, and Jim Rohn.

However, I soon realized that most conferences I attended featured speakers who delivered rehearsed speeches, and I yearned for more than just theoretical knowledge. I understood that achieving my goals required more than mere motivation; I desired to connect with a community of like-minded women unafraid of vulnerability.

During this time, God divinely planted my idea for the Power Woman Experience Conference. This conference would be a safe space for women to share their authentic and unfiltered stories, including the challenges they faced and overcame to succeed in their careers or businesses. The primary goal of this platform was to facilitate the exchange of honest, transformational stories that would inspire and empower other women in attendance. Women could freely and authentically share their insights by creating a supportive and encouraging environment.

Although I faced some initial challenges, I persevered and finally summoned the courage to organize the first Power Woman Experience Conference in Greater Philadelphia in 2017. The event was a resounding success, exceeding my expectations. Attendees were eager to share their stories and experiences, providing each other with valuable tools and resources for career and business growth. The conference fulfilled my vision of creating a supportive and empowering environment where women could freely exchange ideas for upward mobility in their careers and businesses.

At the inaugural event, one of our speakers shared an inspiring story about persistently stirring stagnant waters to uncover hidden treasures. She shared her journey of earning a master's degree from a university outside of the United States, driven by her desire to accelerate her career, fulfill her dreams, and reach the pinnacle of success in the corporate world.

As she contemplated her career trajectory, she realized she needed to return to graduate school to earn a Master's in Business Administration. While researching her preferred graduate school, she discovered that passing the Graduate Management Admission Test (GMAT) was a prerequisite for admission into the MBA program. GMAT is a standardized test designed for individuals seeking admission to graduate schools in the United States.

Despite the challenges, she registered for the GMAT with confidence in her abilities and started studying. After months of intensive preparation, she took the test, hoping for a positive outcome. Unfortunately, to her surprise, when the results were released, she fell short of the required score and received a message from the school rejecting her application. The news was devastating, and she was left shocked and unsure of what to do next.

Amid the setback, she refused to give up on her dreams. In a bold move, she decided to visit the graduate school and negotiate with the dean, even though she was aware of the school's strict admission policies.

Upon arrival, she was met with resistance from the secretary, who insisted that she needed an appointment to see the dean. Undeterred, the woman explained the urgency of her situation and the need to speak with the dean. After some hesitation, the secretary informed the dean, who agreed to meet with her.

"Why are you here?" the dean asked in a friendly tone.

"I am here to request one more chance to retake my GMAT," she responded.

According to her, she told us that the dean paused for a few seconds as if he had never seen such a display of courage before.

"Ma'am, this school has a high standard, and every student must obtain the expected GMAT score before an admission offer can be extended to anyone," the dean stated.

"I understand that, sir. I am asking for just one more chance to retake the GMAT, and I will improve my score," she pleaded.

Our speaker was fortunate that the dean eventually agreed to her request, but there was a catch - she had to achieve the required score within two weeks. She couldn't believe her ears as the dean bent the strictly set rules in her favor, which led her to reflect on what would have happened had she not summoned the boldness to try and negotiate with the dean. If she had just accepted her "fate," she would not have been able to experience the joy of discovering the treasures beneath what she saw on the surface.

In her eagerness to succeed, our speaker rushed home to begin her intense preparation for the retake. She studied fervently, recognizing the importance of achieving the minimum score required for admission. However, despite her efforts, her new results fell below the minimum necessary.

Feeling devastated and completely lost, our speaker considered her limited options. Returning to the dean was not among them since he had already informed her that the retake was her last chance. However, after a few days of contemplation, she summoned the courage to book another appointment to negotiate with the dean. Though a tough call, she realized that the worst-case scenario would be the rejection of her proposal. Trembling with fear in the dean's office, she asked for the opportunity to be a student of the school for just one semester. The dean would then use her performance after the semester to evaluate her ability to meet the rigorous requirements of the MBA program.

The dean's response to our speaker's proposal was positive, granting her the opportunity to attend the school for a semester to prove herself. Our speaker was utterly stunned and grateful for the opportunity, repeatedly pinching herself to confirm that it was not a dream. She attended the school, completed the MBA program and emerged as the best student upon graduation.

She shared her story during the conference to underscore the importance of stirring the stagnant waters. Persistence was the winning edge she needed to achieve her dreams and become a success during that phase of her life.

What is one obstacle in your way? How persistent are you in going after your dreams? Are you the type that does not settle for less, or do you maintain the status quo? To achieve success in life, you must understand the power of persistence. Do not retreat at the slightest show of resistance. You can succeed anywhere you find yourself in the world if you persist in pursuing your desires.

Standing out from the Crowd

Not too long after I graduated from college and got married, my husband and I decided to relocate to the United States of America. Relocating to a new country marked a transition period for us as we also anticipated the arrival of our first child. Packing our belongings, saying goodbye to our families, taking the leap of faith to start anew in a foreign land, and preparing for the birth of a child were all challenges we faced. Nonetheless, we trusted in God's guidance and followed His lead. Shortly after our arrival, our first child was born. While it was a joyous occasion, the aftermath of labor was overwhelming, mainly because I was still recovering from a cesarean section. Consequently, I chose to stay at home so I could fully recuperate.

While still recovering from childbirth, I started my search for a suitable graduate program based on my interest in environmental science. I aimed to pursue a master's degree in environmental and public health. I conducted thorough research and discovered that such a program existed in a graduate school close to home.

Upon reviewing the program details, I found that the application deadline was in January, three months after I came across the information. Although I had many of the application materials ready, I still needed to register for the Graduate Record Examinations (GRE), a standardized test required by many graduate schools, including the school I found close to home.

> "How was I supposed to meet the deadline when I had just given birth, was still recovering from surgery, and had no study materials or guidance?" As I brainstormed my following action, a family friend recommended GRE tutorial classes, but I couldn't afford them.

Several days later, a woman who was aware of the birth of our baby came to our home with gifts. My husband and I were grateful to have people we barely knew extend their love and support to us. The kindness we received from many of the people we met gave us hope that things would turn around for our good.

As we began to unwrap the gifts, we discovered an envelope addressed to us containing $30. The money was the exact amount I needed to purchase a GRE Study Guide since I could not afford to sign up for live classes. With only three months to study, I held my baby in one hand and the study guide in the other, determined to reach my goal.

After three months of studying with the GRE Study Guide, the day finally arrived for me to take the GRE. However, there was one problem - my husband was working, and we couldn't bring our baby to the testing center. I had no other option but to find a babysitter for my child. On the day of the exams, I made my way through the snowy roads of January to drop off my baby at the babysitter before rushing to take the tests.

Meanwhile, when people asked me about my career plans and I revealed my desire to start a career in the environmental industry, I often noticed a look of surprise on their faces. Many of them tried to discourage me from pursuing my dream, not because they thought I couldn't excel but because of their perception that it was an unpopular career path and that it might be challenging to secure a job.

"Why not switch your career to human health?" some people would usually ask suggestively.

"I would like to try environmental science," I would typically respond to them.

Yes, I was determined to continue in the environmental science career path, having invested a significant amount of time and effort, including one year of relevant work experience in the field. Additionally, my research on the prospects of environmental science in a 10-year projection showed promising signs that I was on the right path. With this information in mind, I prepared myself for a successful career by studying hard and trusting God to guide me as I remained committed to my career choice.

After a week of writing my exams, I checked my results and was thrilled to discover that I had met the minimum requirements. It felt like I had won the lottery because studying for the GRE had been demanding. I was relieved that my effort had yielded satisfactory results and felt highly optimistic about receiving the letter of admission from the school. In February, I got the exciting news that I had been offered admission to graduate school! This news represented another victory for me and established that it is hardly worthwhile to follow the crowd.

Conforming to popular opinions often has adverse outcomes, as others' beliefs and preferences sway individuals. Had I followed the suggestions regarding my career path, I can only imagine how different my life would be now. However, I am fulfilled because my career choices resulted from my decisions. If I had heeded the advice of others, things could have gone wrong, and I may have blamed them for my misfortunes.

Furthermore, I have noticed that my energy level is always higher when I pursue things I choose for myself rather than those others suggest.

In high school, one of my favorite quotes from my teachers was, "The crowd is mostly wrong." And I agree with it. What's funny about the crowd is that they'll still blame you if you follow them and things don't work out as planned. Therefore, to live a happy and fulfilling life, you should strive to make decisions based on your convictions rather than popular opinion. This philosophy is essential if you want to achieve important things in life. Just because everyone does something in a particular way doesn't mean it's the right way.

My offer of admission was for the Fall semester, so I had a few months before the start of classes. While waiting, I continued to encounter people who seemed genuinely worried about my career choice and subtly pressured me to consider other options. For instance, one of my acquaintances appeared to be the most concerned. According to her, she was confident that I was on the wrong path and that I ought to have heeded her voice of reason.

"I studied economics while in college, but now I am back in school to join the health profession," she declared during our discussion.

On the one hand, her words ran deep. On the other hand, I was convinced I made the right choice. I had made considerable progress on that path and could not afford to look back. Then, one day, as I went grocery shopping, I heard through the grapevine that my acquaintance had abandoned the health profession program to enroll in a new school for a Master of Business Administration (MBA). At first, I thought it was a mistaken identity until I called to confirm the news and congratulated her.

> "I am sorry I did not inform you earlier," she swiftly chipped in.

She then told me how unhappy she was and had to consider changing careers. She felt she was living an unfulfilled life, which led her to look inward and find answers to this pertinent question: "How can I live a fulfilled life?" I was happy that she retraced her steps. For your information, she is doing great today.

Generally speaking, as you journey in life, you'll encounter people who always have an opinion about what they think you should or should not do. However, the ball is in your court, and you can play it whichever way you like. Playing your ball in the direction of popular opinions rather than based on personal conviction can lead to unintended consequences which may be irreversible or costly. If you want to achieve success in life, against all odds, you must develop the ability to stand alone when the occasion calls for it. Please do not follow the crowd; stand out from them.

Experiencing a Glorious Moment

The offer of admission I received was for full-time enrollment, which I intended to pursue. I planned to complete my master's degree in less than two years to accelerate my career. However, I later discovered that all classes were scheduled at night regardless of enrollment status. The nightly schedule left me wondering what I would do during the day, as I was not used to having idle time.

As a wife and mother, my goal was to secure employment in a reputable firm or organization that would allow me to achieve excellent results while still being able to prioritize my family. I clearly understood the type of job I wanted, the responsibilities I would take on, and the work environment I desired. However, due to a lack of internet access, compiling a list of potential employers took a lot of work.

One day, during a brainstorming session, God reminded me of the environmental organization where I retrieved data I used to support my results from my undergraduate capstone experiment and project. Excitedly, I shared the idea with my husband, who promised to look it up during his next visit to the local library since we had no internet access at home. I had to wait until he went to the library patiently, and when he eventually did, he came back with an abundance of information for both of us.

While at the library, my husband discovered that the environmental organization only hired US citizens. However, from his research, he found another environmental organization that matched my requirements. He returned home that day with paper applications which took several hours to complete. We both filled out the applications happily, posting them through the mail, hoping for the best.

Back then, there was no immediate confirmation from employers as to your application status, unlike today, where you can track the status of your application at the click of a button. So, all I did was hope and pray for a positive outcome.

While waiting, I constantly experienced discouragement from people who continued to advise me without fail on the need to give up on my dream of securing a professional job in the environmental field. I stood my ground, refused to let go of my hope and continued believing that something great would come from my expectations.

After several weeks of waiting, my anxiety about the status of my application had reached its peak. However, one day, as my husband returned from work, he handed me a letter with my name on it. I quickly opened the envelope and was overjoyed to see that it contained a confirmation receipt for my application and an invitation to an interview!

Receiving this letter was a significant moment for me as it reinforced my belief that my aspirations were attainable if I remained determined and took the necessary steps to make them a reality. As a child growing up in Rock City's suburbs, pursuing my dreams and seeing them come to fruition seemed like an unattainable fantasy. So, I was thrilled at the prospect of attending the interview, and the excitement filled me with a renewed sense of purpose and drive.

Once the initial excitement had subsided, I realized that I had no backup plan as I had put all my eggs in one basket and decided to give my all to prepare for the upcoming interview. With a determined spirit, I resolved to leave no stone unturned as I honed my skills and knowledge.

As I delved into my preparations, I thoroughly covered all bases, including researching the company and position. Additionally, I meticulously planned my route to the organization, considering every possible mode of transportation.

To my pleasant surprise, I discovered that the office was conveniently accessible by train, which filled me with a sense of comfort and reassurance. This realization felt like a sign that God was guiding me toward the right path and that I was on the right track toward achieving my dreams.

As I took a closer look at the job description, I couldn't help but feel an overwhelming sense of gratitude and appreciation for the opportunity that lay before me. As an immigrant, I was well aware of the challenges of securing a job aligned with my vision, making this opportunity all the more significant. The position was a perfect fit for my career goals and aspirations, and the offered benefits and flexibility were a bonus.

On the day of the interview, I was determined to make a lasting impression and give it my all. I answered every question to the best of my ability, drawing on my previous experiences and knowledge to showcase my skills and expertise. The interview went smoothly, and I left feeling confident in my performance. However, as the waiting game began, I couldn't shake off the nervousness and excitement that consumed me. I couldn't help but wonder if I had said everything I needed to say and if I had presented myself in the best possible light. The thought of receiving a job offer was both exhilarating and daunting simultaneously, as I knew it would be a life-changing opportunity to set me on the path toward achieving my dreams.

Undergoing a Period of Waiting

As the days turned into weeks, my anticipation for a response from the potential employer grew stronger. I constantly checked my phone and email, hoping for any updates. However, as time passed, the waiting period seemed to drag on forever, and doubts started to creep in. Despite my efforts to stay positive, I began to worry that I may not have performed below the cutoff.

Despite my efforts to stay busy, the wait weighed on my mind. I researched more about the company and the role I interviewed for to distract myself from the delay. I wanted to be fully prepared; perhaps they contacted me for a second interview or to discuss the terms of my employment.

A few weeks had passed since my interview, but it felt like an eternity. I had not received any word regarding my employment status, which confused me about what to do next. After much contemplation, I decided to pluck up the courage and call the human resource specialist, my point of contact.

Determined, I picked up the phone and made the call, hoping for a positive outcome. Although I was nervous, I knew that I needed to take control of the situation and get some clarity on my employment status. After all, I had worked hard to prepare for the interview and felt I deserved to know where I stood.

When the phone was answered, I said, "Hello, my name is Seun Akinlotan. I was interviewed for a position at your office a few weeks ago and am calling to check back with you." However, the response I received from the other end of the line differed from what I had hoped for. A male voice calmly told me he was not privy to my interview status.

This response left me feeling disappointed. However, I remained hopeful and focused on other activities to keep myself occupied. I continued researching and networking to prepare for potential job opportunities, and I also worked on my personal development by taking courses and engaging in hobbies.

"Hoping to get a call back is delusional," a woman told me after she learned about the interview. According to her, once a prospective employer goes silent for over a month, it is the employer's way of saying, "Forget about the job."

Thankfully, her words had almost no impact on me as I had seen God in action several times, so I refused to let go of my faith and hope in God. I continued to call the office daily to check for any updates on my application. The human resource specialist got used to my persistent calls, and he recognized my voice every time I called. Finally, when I had almost given up hope, I received a call offering me the job.

The joy and relief I felt were beyond words as I thanked God for coming through for me yet again. I realized that my faith and perseverance had paid off. I had held on to God's promises for my life, and he had not disappointed me. It reminded me that all things are possible with God, even in the face of discouragement and delay. I was grateful for the experience as it taught me to trust God's timing and plans for my life.

It was one of the most defining moments of my life as it jump-started my career as an environmentalist in the United States. The waiting period was over, although not without its challenges and the lessons of life that would later prove beneficial!

What Are You Waiting on God for?

Regardless of what you may be waiting on God for - whether it is for career advancement, a new job opportunity, a successful exam, a life partner, or even a child - it is important to remember that God is faithful and capable of doing the impossible. No matter how big or small your desires may seem, they are valid and worthy of pursuit.

Waiting on God can be challenging, especially when time is running out, or nothing is happening. However, during the season of waiting, you must hold on to your faith and trust that God's timing is perfect. He may not always answer our prayers in the way or time you expect, but He knows what is best for us and will never leave or forsake you.

As you wait on God, you must not give in to doubt, fear, or discouragement. Instead, believe with all your heart that things will turn out in your favor. Be sure to take practical steps towards your goals while being patient and allowing God to work in His time. Keep trusting in Him, believing, and waiting with hope and expectation.

Who Do You Listen to While Waiting?

As you wait on God for your breakthrough, you must be mindful of who you allow into your life. Bishop T.D. Jakes once said, "You cannot rebuke a devil that you continuously grant access to your life." This quote means that if you allow harmful and toxic people into your inner circle without being intentional, they can have a significant impact on your life. The people you allow into your life have the power to influence you with their words and actions. If you surround yourself with individuals who are always negative and sow seeds of discouragement, it can be challenging to maintain a positive outlook on your situation. Therefore, being mindful of the people you grant access to your life is crucial.

One way to be intentional about who you allow into your life is by setting boundaries. Identify the people who consistently bring negativity into your life and limit your interactions with them. Instead, surround yourself with individuals who will support and encourage you in your journey.

Remember, your dreams are valid; waiting on God requires faith and patience. Don't let negative people derail you from your path to success. Trust in God, stay focused and surround yourself with positive and supportive individuals who will help you achieve your goals.

What Are You Doing While Waiting?

One of my favorite quotes is, "The period of waiting is a period of preparation and not lamentation." This quote has been ingrained in my heart since high school and still guides me today. However, I must admit that waiting is challenging, especially when you are still determining the outcome. And if you are not careful, you may start engaging in unproductive activities.

What, then, should you be doing while you wait? Of a truth, I have had a fair share of this critical period in life — waiting for different things in different seasons — yet I have come to terms with the reality that preparation is one of the best activities anybody can engage in. I encourage you to follow suit. If you ever find yourself waiting, take advantage of the available opportunities to prepare for what you wait for rather than simply folding your arms.

In my work, I encounter numerous individuals who, rather than diligently preparing for a bright future, opt for the treacherous path of idleness. Consequently, when the long-awaited opportunity emerges from the shadows, they need more time to grasp it with the full force it deserves. But my message to you is this: Do not follow in their footsteps.

The time is now to shatter the shackles of complacency, rise above the crowd, and forge an unwavering determination toward the brilliance that awaits.

If you are waiting to receive feedback from a job interview, start preparing for your anticipated role. Refrain from focusing solely on remuneration. Instead, devote your time to learning about your role and making plans to add value to the organization. Visit the company's website to learn more about its mission, vision, and core values.

If you are a business owner waiting to transact with your first client, prepare by implementing efficient systems and processes to help you deliver superb customer service. Decide how you want to serve the client, have all your ducks in a row, and be ready to hit the ground running. Whatever it is, prepare as much as possible while you wait.

Digging out the Gold Mine

Many years ago, I read the exciting story of a tourist who visited a village and saw a young boy playing with what looked like a dirty rock. He asked the boy's mom whether the gem had any value, and she said no. This tourist was curious nonetheless and asked for permission to have the rock sampled. In a nutshell, it was not an ordinary stone but a piece of gold! That was how gold mining started in a tiny village.

Up until the time of the discovery, most residents were living below the poverty line! Such is life. Isn't it? We all sit on treasures daily yet fail to see and use them. It's the same way we are all loaded with the gifts that can move us from struggling to thriving, but the major problem is being unable to recognize them. In other words, our inability to tap into our potential or mine the gold deposited in us limits us. In one of her books, Joyce Meyer writes, "Potential is a priceless treasure, like gold. We all have gold hidden within, but we must dig to get it out." This quote is nothing but the truth.

Stirring the Stagnant Waters

Most times, ignorance is the reason we never move forward. A lot of people lack the zeal to fight complacency. They are always laid-back, comfortable with living an average lifestyle, prefer to complain and give excuses, and, worse still, blame everyone and everything but themselves. Whereas all they need is just quality information — although right under their nose — that will lead them to their breakthroughs. No need to run "kiti kiti kata-kata" here and there for supposed solutions as quick fixes. Some even harbor the self-limiting belief that they cannot make it in life without traveling to other locations. Meanwhile, they possess the talents that can make them succeed right where they are.

> The Yorubas have a famous adage that
> perfectly depicts situations like this,
> and it can be loosely translated:
> "What you are going to look for in Sokoto is
> right inside the pockets of your sokoto."

This adage means that you have all the resources you need to excel right where you are if you only take the time to look deeper. God is so concerned about us that He made available all the resources needed to cater to our needs. Most times, all you need to do is ask Him in prayers, and He will answer you.

Take a careful look at the bible story of how Jesus fed the crowd while his disciples were thinking of going far into a city to look for food or even sending the crowd away to go and get food to eat. Jesus looked within and multiplied the available resources. The resources we need are always within reach, but we must look inward before maximizing them. Those resources are our goldmine, and all that is expected of us is to mine it!

Do not wait to be spoon-fed. You are already sitting on a goldmine, so start digging. Stay within a reasonable distance looking for what has been readily available for you. Just look around; most of what you need is already provided. Ask yourself today, "What treasures am I sitting on?" It is time to quit being complacent and begin to explore the gold mine you are sitting on.

Recognizing the Winning Edge

At the beginning of my career as an environmental scientist, I found myself in a mentally taxing season of life. This was the same month I had started graduate school, and I felt stretched beyond my capacity. I juggled many responsibilities as a wife, mom, immigrant, worker, and student. It was overwhelming, but I was determined to make it work.

One day after work, while waiting for the train, I used the quiet office space to catch up on some school reading. I had only been studying for about half an hour when I heard a voice behind me. It was one of my coworkers who was curious about why I was still in my cubicle at that time of the day. I explained to him that I had decided to study while I waited for the train.

"Are you trying to become my supervisor one day?" he asked inquisitively.

The encounter with my coworker left me feeling unsettled and uncomfortable. I was unsure how to react to his statement, as it came out of nowhere. As a new employee, I was pressured to adjust to a new job and manage multiple responsibilities. I couldn't understand why he would assume I would become his supervisor and was at a loss for words and unsure how to react. I hoped he would realize his comment's inappropriate and walk away. However, he continued to explain his frustrations and reasons for his statement. I was taken aback by his remarks and struggled to process the encounter.

Afterward, I talked about the situation with my husband and parents. Their support and encouragement helped me to feel settled. I realized that I couldn't control other people's reactions and opinions, but I could focus on doing my best in my job and continuing to learn and grow.

A few years passed, and nothing happened in my career regarding promotion. This was because of the need for more opportunities for advancement that matched my criteria. I was clear about where I desired to be, but taking care of my family was my top priority. I rejected the job offers that would take me away from my family, even when they came with attractive compensation packages. However, I kept my eyes and options open.

Interestingly, a competitive management opportunity with the potential for promotion opened up when I least expected it. Upon reviewing the qualifications required for the position, I threw my hat in the ring. To secure the coveted role, I had to contend with other candidates. The rigorous interview process involved a pool of around ten applicants, including my colleague, who had declared that he would resign if I became his supervisor. Despite the initial competition, only four of us remained after the screening. The interview was intense, and we all felt uncertain about the outcome. However, after the interview, we eagerly waited for the results, but unfortunately, our employer made no announcements regarding the developments.

> "Hope deferred," as the saying
> goes, "makes the heart sick."

Six months passed after the interview, and with no feedback, my interest waned. In the eighth month, our employer announced the reopening of the role, and interested parties were invited to submit new applications, including those of us who had applied previously. Despite feeling discouraged, my husband urged me to give it another shot.

> "What is the worst that can happen?" I recall him asking me.

The worst that could happen was that I would not be selected for the position, others might get chosen, or the hiring manager would leave the role empty if no one were competent enough. Whichever way, I had nothing to lose but everything to gain. Conversely, if I got called for the interview and selected, that would be good for me. And even if I participated and ended up not being chosen, it would still be to my advantage because I would have gained more insights into the interview process for supervisory roles.

So, with my husband's support and encouragement, I reapplied for the position and started preparing for the interview. While waiting to be called, I asked myself serious questions: "What is my winning edge?" "What can I do or say to help me stand out among the applicants?"

To answer the question, I reflected on how I had prepared and equipped myself over the years. My edge came from a combination of factors, including my dedication to preparation, willingness to take risks in uncharted territories, and constant hunger for knowledge. One of the ways I set myself apart was by attending training sessions regularly. I invested in myself and attended more training programs than the average worker. While my employer sponsored some of these programs, I also paid for many of them out of pocket. This commitment to ongoing education and self-improvement proved invaluable in preparing me for my new role.

Furthermore, my skills in strategy and design allowed me to develop a clear vision for how I intended to manage the new role. I had thought about this extensively and had ideas about improving the organization and making it more successful. This level of planning and preparation gave me an edge in the interview process and ultimately helped me secure the position.

Just two weeks after submitting my application for the position, I received an invitation for an interview, which was much faster than I had anticipated. Following the interview, I was delighted to learn that I had been selected for the role after only another two weeks. It felt like a stroke of luck, and I was overwhelmed with joy. I felt as though God had blessed me at a time when I least expected it. It was surreal to see my coworker's prediction of me becoming his supervisor come to fruition so quickly. As I witnessed it all unfold, I couldn't help but believe it was a divine orchestration.

A few days after the announcement of my new position in the organization, I was settling into my new office when I heard a knock on the door. Upon turning around, I saw my colleague standing before me. He had come to congratulate me on my promotion and expressed his commitment to supporting me as my direct report. The encounter was emotional, and I was amazed at how things had turned out. It starkly contrasted his comments several years prior, which I had held close to my heart. I thanked him for his kind words and support, but I couldn't shake the memory of his previous statements.

Call to Action

◊ Take time to observe and learn the rules of any new environment you find yourself in, whether a school, church, workplace or even a country.

◊ Executing any project or plan successfully requires excellent clarity. Therefore, plan what you want to research or achieve and how much time and resources it will need.

◊ Be prepared to make your case when faced with unexpected challenges or setbacks. Sometimes, explaining your position and creating a solid argument can help you overcome obstacles.

◊ Keep asking, seeking, and knocking when pursuing a goal or dream, push forward, and never give up.

◊ Trust in God's guidance, follow his prompts in challenging situations, and believe that things will turn out in your favor, no matter what you are waiting for.

◊ Do not be afraid to pursue your goals and dreams — even if it means taking a less popular career path — avoid following the crowd mindlessly.

◊ Apply for that position but research the company and the role. Be relentless and follow up on your job application.

◊ Maximize the waiting period for preparation, not lamentation.

- CHAPTER EIGHT -

Understanding Cultures

"Your success in today's globalized world requires an ability to adapt to a variety of cultural situations."

David Livermore

When my family's healthcare practitioner learned about our intended relocation to the United States, he posed a crucial question that I had not yet considered: "Have you familiarized yourself with the basics of American culture?" This question caught me off guard, as I had not thought about how American culture might affect my family and me once we moved, nor had I considered how to prepare for the transition. When I admitted to him that I had not considered it, he gave me an impromptu lesson on the fundamentals of American culture. Our discussion centered mainly on religion, parenting, and the concept of the American dream.

After that initial conversation, I became curious about American culture and researched it more extensively. To my surprise, volunteering is a fundamental aspect of American society. My finding starkly contrasted with my upbringing in Nigeria, where many considered volunteering insignificant. Many people believed that it was impossible to volunteer without receiving some form of compensation. The culture was centered around receiving payment for services rendered. However, in America, the opposite was and still is true. Patriotism and selflessness are core values instilled in most Americans from childhood, and giving back to the community through volunteering is a highly valued activity. This discovery was eye-opening and helped me better understand my new home's culture.

Equipped with this newfound knowledge about the importance of volunteering in American culture and fueled by my inherent desire to help others, I fully embraced this culture. I became involved in causes that aligned with my values upon my relocation. This decision proved to be a significant turning point for me as it opened up numerous doors of opportunity that I never could have imagined. Looking back, had I not taken the time to understand the importance of volunteering in American culture, my career growth would have likely been slower. By embracing this culture, I was able to build a strong network, develop new skills, and make a positive impact in my community, all of which have helped to propel my career forward.

Culture is the integrated pattern of human knowledge, belief, and behavior that depends on the capacity for learning and transmitting knowledge to succeeding generations. In the context of readily adapting to a new environment, David Livermore calls it the cultural intelligence quotient (CQ) in one of his books,

> "The Cultural Intelligence Difference." He notes that CQ "is the capability to function effectively across various cultural contexts, such as ethnic, generational, and organizational cultures."

If you want to succeed against all odds, it is imperative that you intentionally master the fundamentals of the culture of the location you find yourself. Whether in the workplace, an organization, or a new country especially, understanding the existing culture will give you an edge.

In August 2016, Mark Zuckerberg, the co-founder, and CEO of Meta Platforms (formerly Facebook, Inc.), visited Nigeria unexpectedly. During his visit, he was spotted at a local cafeteria sitting on a bench and eating yam flour pudding with his right hand, without any utensils. This public display endeared him to many Nigerians, who saw his gesture as genuine, down-to-earth, and approachable.

In addition to his casual dining experience, Zuckerberg's itinerary included a meeting with the president of Nigeria and other high-ranking officials. As news of his visit spread online, thought leaders on social media sparked a debate about what he would wear to the meeting. Known for his preference for casual attire, some speculated that he would maintain his usual style, while others believed that he would dress formally. The variety of opinions generated significant anticipation for the outcome of the meeting.

When he met with the Nigerian president, Mark Zuckerberg appeared to have consciously decided to forego his usual casual attire instead of dressing formally in a white shirt, maroon tie, and black blazer. Zukerberg's departure from his typical preference for casual clothing showed that he recognized the importance of respecting and embracing the culture of the location he visited, and he did so in a way that made his visit significant.

By dressing formally for the meeting, Zuckerberg demonstrated his willingness to adapt to the cultural norms. It was a small gesture, but the act also spoke volumes about his respect and ability to adjust to a new environment. Zuckerberg's actions suggested that he took time to learn more about Nigerian culture, which was essential to building meaningful relationships and creating positive change.

Delving into the intricacies of culture is akin to embarking on a fascinating expedition, where we immerse ourselves in the essence of an environment and master the art of adaptation. Through this profound understanding, we unlock the key to forging genuine connections with those who call that place home. By embracing and integrating the indispensable facets of their culture, we accelerate our personal growth and pave a fast track toward triumph and prosperity. So, dare to venture beyond the surface, unravel the mysteries, and harness the power of cultural comprehension to propel yourself toward unparalleled progress and resounding success.

Transport yourself back to when the digital realm was still a privileged domain and internet access was a rare commodity. I was in the hot seat during this era, interviewing for a coveted job opportunity. Little did I know that the question awaiting me would unleash a profound clash of cultures. As a proud bearer of Nigerian heritage, ingrained with values discouraging self-promotion, I was suddenly confronted with the demand to tout my merits. It felt like traversing unfamiliar terrain, teetering on the precipice of discomfort. Yet, as the sands of time shifted beneath my feet, I came to a powerful realization: In America, the land of opportunity, mastering the art of self-promotion is a crucial skill, particularly in the fiercely competitive job search landscape.

In the fiercely competitive job landscape, you are left with no choice but to blow your own horn, albeit with a touch of humility. It's a reality we must face: you must showcase your achievements and unique qualities to avoid being overshadowed by candidates whose qualifications may not even hold a candle to yours. But here's the catch: understanding cultural norms continues once you've secured the job. No, it's only the beginning. Once you land the job, you'll need to learn to navigate the intricate web of cultural norms and practices within your newfound environment to unlock a seamless integration and unparalleled comfort.

Adapting to a new culture can also help make others feel more comfortable around you. It shows you are respectful, open-minded, and willing to learn and adapt to new environments. Adapting to a new culture can be especially important when starting a new job or moving to a new community, where integrating into the system can be crucial for success.

Understanding and embracing a place's culture can significantly impact one's personal and professional life. One aspect of the culture that I have come to master in my current residence is joining my coworkers for lunch. Although I'm not particularly fond of eating out, I make it a point to attend these social gatherings after work. It's an opportunity to learn more about my colleagues beyond the work environment, and it has proven to be an invaluable way to expand my network and career opportunities.

During these outings, I gained insight into exciting job prospects and learned about the people being considered for various roles. Showing up at these events has increased my visibility and helped me establish meaningful connections with my colleagues. Failing to understand the culture of a place can lead to missed opportunities, isolation, and overall dissatisfaction.

It is, however, important to note that In the captivating tapestry of cultural exploration, it's essential to tread with discernment. Understanding a culture doesn't entail mindlessly conforming to its practices; instead, it involves embarking on a voyage of observation and learning. From the subtle nuances of greetings to the tantalizing flavors of local cuisine and the vibrant attire, every aspect offers a window into the rich tapestry of a community's customs. By immersing yourself in this journey of discovery, you can unveil a treasure trove of traditions, sifting through them to discern the ones that resonate with your values and sensibilities. This delicate process empowers you to weave a personalized tapestry of cultural integration, embracing the practices that harmonize with your identity and beliefs.

I must, however, admit that understanding a culture can be challenging. Being in a new environment is daunting for most people, and learning to catch up with the system can also be overwhelming. However, if you commit to understanding the culture of a new environment, it is an effective means of accelerating your progress in that place. Adapting takes keeping an open mind to learn new experiences, the courage to persevere when things fail to happen the way you want, and the temerity to keep going no matter what happens.

Eliminating Guesswork

Adapting to a new environment can be a daunting experience, especially if you are unfamiliar with the customs, traditions, and expectations of the people in that unique setting. Cutting corners and skipping the due process can be tempting to save time and effort, but this can lead to costly mistakes and unfavorable outcomes. Instead, it is essential to take the time to learn about the culture, understand what is acceptable and what is not, and apply this knowledge to your daily interactions.

When you rely on facts and data rather than assumptions, you can increase the accuracy and efficiency of your work. Data helps you to avoid costly mistakes and to work more effectively with greater confidence. By applying general principles, you can produce more reliable results, reduce risks, and make informed choices that benefit your career growth and personal development.

One practical way to integrate quickly into a new setting is to gather relevant data and information, observe how people behave, interact, communicate, and learn from their experiences. Doing this helps you to identify opportunities and potential roadblocks and to develop strategies that enable you to adapt successfully to your new environment. Ultimately, taking the time to understand the culture of a place and applying this knowledge to your interactions is critical to your success in any new environment.

Understanding Cultures

Cultivating a Flexible Attitude

In the first year, I started working; it took me some time to understand the culture and integrate myself into the new system. The office culture was divergent from what I was accustomed to, and aligning myself became an uphill battle.

On Mondays, people would show up at work, and the first thing they often did was chit-chat. "How about settling in first?" I would wonder. How you start your Monday determines how the rest of the workweek will pan out. Therefore, I preferred to begin Mondays by setting achievable weekly goals instead of chatting away with my coworkers.

After a while, I observed that the more I stayed away from the chit-chat, the farther I drifted into isolation. That was different than the way to go if I would ever feel like I belonged there. Although it took me a long time, I worked on my mindset and rearranged my schedule to participate in casual conversations at work. The saying goes,

"When in Rome, do as the Romans do."

For instance, before settling into my workspace to kick-start the work for the day, I would chat with others for a few minutes. Rather than waiting until Monday morning before setting realistic goals for the week, I also ensured that I started planning for Mondays before leaving the office on Friday. This strategy freed up a little bit of my time on Mondays and allowed for chit-chat. In fact, with this simple act, I saw life differently from others, that is, understanding my coworkers' perspectives. Of course, I only realized that once I embraced their culture.

Adopting this flexible attitude marked a turning point, and it allowed me to deeply connect with a new set of people without losing myself in the process. It is about being an outsider and fitting well into a new environment in a way that makes those who got there before me comfortable. It created a win-win situation.

Each time you find yourself in a new country, the workplace, a group, or an organization, be open-minded and seek to learn how things are being done there. Observe how people interact with one another, study their language, either implicitly or explicitly, and start mingling with them in a manner that puts them at ease.

Once you start doing this, people will certainly let you in on favorable opportunities because they will naturally think of you first, especially when you are qualified. Understanding culture and cultivating a flexible attitude toward it are winning strategies in breaking down barriers in that setting, thus leading to extraordinary success for you.

Reading the Fine Print

Many years ago, I attended a high-profile conference that lasted for a week. As an avid learner, I was excited about the opportunity to learn and improve my skills. More importantly, the conference allowed me to enjoy peace without the usual disruptions of being a family woman.

Walking into my hotel room, I noticed a bottle of purified water sitting on the table. The bottle had a tag around its neck that said, "Drink for life." It was a nice touch from the hotel to provide water for their guests, and I made it a habit to drink one bottle each day, as it was replenished daily by the room service staff.

Little did I know that the "Drink for life" tag was more than just a catchy slogan, as I received an invoice from the hotel indicating that I had been billed $25 for consuming five bottles of water on the last day. Astonished, I called the help desk and was informed that each water bottle cost $5.

"No one told me each water bottle costs $5," I retorted.

"Well, the price of the water has a sign around the bottle," the personnel responded.

Understanding Cultures

I almost argued the fact until I paid attention to the sign. Apart from the tag containing the bold inscription I first saw, the hotel included the price in the fine print section — which I failed to read!

Was it ethical for the hotel to do that? That is up in the air! Life, like the sign hung over the water bottles I drank each day, is filled with offers and opportunities that come with the fine print.

The experience of being charged $25 for five bottles of water during a hotel stay taught me a valuable lesson about paying attention to details. It can be easy to overlook important information when we assume things are straightforward and make assumptions based on our expectations and experiences.

In this case, the "Drink for life" tag on the water bottle initially led me to assume that the water was provided as a complimentary amenity. I should have taken the time to read the fine print and noticed that the price of each bottle was $5. This mistake led to an unexpected and unwelcome charge on my hotel bill.

The incident serves as a reminder that it is always important to pay attention to details, especially when dealing with unfamiliar environments or situations. Reading instructions, signs, and other information carefully can help us avoid costly mistakes and make better-informed decisions.

Always devote the time to read the fine print before jumping at an offer because it could contain important information that may affect your decision to accept or decline the offer.

Here is some information that may be embedded in the fine print:

⋄ **Hidden terms and conditions:** The fine print often contains detailed terms and conditions that may take time to decipher from the main offer. They may include restrictions, qualifications, or exclusions that could limit the offer's benefits or impose additional costs or obligations on the user.

◊ **Expiration dates:** The fine print may also contain information about the offer's expiration date. You must use the offer before expiration to ensure you get all the benefits.

◊ **Fees**: The fine print may disclose fees or charges associated with the offer. For example, a credit card may offer a zero percent interest rate for the first six months but then charge a high-interest rate after that period. By reading the fine print, you can understand the total cost of the offer and make an informed decision.

◊ **Specific requirements:** The fine print may have specific requirements that you must meet to qualify for the offer. For example, a cashback offer may require a minimum purchase amount, or a travel offer may allow you to book a certain number of nights in a hotel. By reading the fine print, you can know whether you meet the requirements for the offer.

If you want to overcome the challenges associated with integrating into a new environment and clearly understand its culture, be sure to study the inner workings of that environment in detail, which can be likened to the fine print.

Attention to the fine print will save you from pitfalls, missed opportunities, or other surprises that could negatively impact your experience in a new setting. Therefore, take the time to understand the culture you find yourself in to make informed decisions, integrate seamlessly and achieve success against all odds.

Call to Action

◊ Take time to research the culture of a new environment and learn about the beliefs, values, and behaviors the people subscribe to over there.

◊ Identify the part of the culture that aligns with your values and beliefs, and try to incorporate them into your life.

◊ Be observant. Take note of how things are done in the new culture, including how people greet, eat, worship, or dress, and pick something you are comfortable with to make everyone comfortable.

◊ Participate in social events, even if they are outside of your comfort zone. This will help you learn more about the people you work with or live close to and increase your visibility for future opportunities.

◊ Embrace the culture of your new workplace, and adapt without losing your essence. Eliminate guesswork and rely on facts and correct data to avoid making errors.

◊ Devote time to reading the fine print, especially when an offer is given out of the blue, to ensure that you are fully aware of the terms and conditions of the offer.

- CHAPTER NINE -

From Setbacks to Stepping Up

"Setbacks are inevitable; misery is a choice."

Stephen R. Covey

Accepting a job offer from an organization I have always dreamed about, only for the offer to be rescinded, was a bitter experience I have had to live through. How would you react if you received a job offer from an organization you have always dreamed of working at, and that decision was reversed a few weeks after? Here is the full story:

I got the news of the offer being withdrawn on a Friday afternoon as I was returning home from a trip to the supposedly "soon-to-be" workplace.

"I am calling to let you know that we are no longer interested in bringing you on board," the personnel manager casually told me.

At first, I thought it was a prank, but as we went deeper into the conversation, I realized I had lost the opportunity.

Once the personnel manager dropped the phone, I wept uncontrollably and sweated profusely inside the train as different thoughts raced through my mind. How could God allow this to happen to me? How would I return to the workplace where everyone thought I was leaving? What explanation would I offer to my teammates who took me out for lunch to honor my intended exit? How about the other employees gearing up to take on my position once I exit?

Getting an interview at the organization took me several years of trying and when I finally thought my moment to step up had finally arrived, I was dealt another cruel blow.

I became highly disappointed in myself and how things had turned out throughout the weekend.

Eventually, when I returned to the office the following week to inform them of the disappointment I had met at the organization I had applied, the enthusiastic support I received was unprecedented, especially from my managers. One of them took it upon himself to make some phone calls on my behalf while boosting my morale as he offered great counsel and encouragement.

In a separate encounter, a co-worker stopped me in the hallway a few weeks after the incident and said, "Seun, you are like a little child who falls down and immediately gets up to keep going." I smiled while responding because I knew he was surprised at my remarkable ability to keep moving despite the setback.

As I continued to perform my roles, I focused on honing report writing skills, including taking up more complex tasks that many others would rather sidestep. I used the setback as a learning experience and did not allow it to deter me from showing up and doing my best at my duty post.

The following year, an opportunity was created for stepping up at work, although unexpectedly. When I reviewed the requirements, I discovered I met most, if not all, of them. That was a thrilling moment for me, but I erred on the side of caution due to my previous experience with the organization I had applied to, not to mention the competitive nature of other co-workers who were also interested in advancing. In the end, I competed against 11 people, and I was a successful candidate. I was elated to have seized the opportunity, especially when it dawned on me, in retrospect, that my initial setback was indeed a blessing in disguise.

Dealing with Setbacks in Life

Learn from my experience. I am unsure of the setbacks you have experienced or are currently experiencing in your life, but over time I have developed some strategies for dealing with setbacks. In the heat of the moment, you may feel overwhelmed, disappointed, or defeated, but the steps you take during such a difficult period will determine whether you will come out of it as a better person.

◊ **Acknowledge your emotions:** Feeling upset, disappointed, or frustrated after a setback is okay. Acknowledge and accept these feelings, and give yourself time to process them. Do not live in denial

◊ **Practice self-compassion:** Be kind and compassionate toward yourself. Choose not to beat yourself up over the setback. Instead, focus on what you can learn from the experience and how you can use that knowledge to move forward.

◊ **Reframe the setback:** Try to see the setback as an opportunity for growth and learning. Ask yourself what you can learn from the experience and how you can use this knowledge to improve.

⋄ **Take a break:** Sometimes, taking a break from the situation can help you gain a new perspective and come back with an enlightened mindset. Take some time to do something you enjoy or engage in self-care activities.

⋄ **Seek support:** Do not be afraid to contact friends, family, or a mental health professional. Sometimes, talking to someone can help you process your emotions and gain a new perspective.

⋄ **Stay focused on your goals:** Setbacks can be discouraging, but do not let them derail you from your goals. Stay focused on your long-term objectives and take small daily steps to achieve them. Marcus Aurelius, in Meditations, states, "A rational being can turn each setback into raw material and use it to achieve its goal." Yes, have this mindset at all times.

⋄ **Ask God to help you keep things in perspective:** It is important to remember that setbacks are a natural part of the journey toward success. Try to keep things in perspective, and remember that setbacks do not reflect your worth or abilities.

Seeing Rejection as a Catalyst

In October 2022, a popular design platform called Canva hit the news when it was announced that the website had attained a significant milestone of having 100 million monthly active users.

As a content creator, I always need great designs that I can easily create at the click of a button. So when I discovered Canva in 2017, I was pleased with the ease of using the platform. I also noticed a series of constant improvements on the platform, which awakened my curiosity to learn more about the soul behind the brand. That was how I found out about Melanie Perkins, the CEO and co-founder of Canva.

Ms. Perkins is an Australian-based tech founder who launched the Canva idea from her mum's living room. Her main goal was to create a platform where designers and non-designers could easily create digital designs on the open web. As the brand grew, she identified the need to raise money from investors to expand.

Of course, raising money was not a walk in the park in those days, as more than 100 investors rejected her. While waiting for a YES from at least one investor, she and her co-founder kept the hope alive without losing enthusiasm. In 2013 she finally got the YES and started building Canva as a one-stop design platform for people with little technical or design skills!

Her story struck me most in her ability to stay the course during the waiting period. Despite numerous rejections that seemed like an eternity, she kept at it. Today, she has built a billion-dollar brand with over 3,920 employees. The ability to withstand multiple rejections without losing enthusiasm is an incredible feat for a woman under 40.

Imagine if she had quit after a few rejections, or perhaps if she had switched to something else during her waiting period; what would have happened to the brand today? The waiting period is a time of patience, foresight, and focus. Patience is needed to stay the course when you reach the point where your dreams will never see the light of day, while foresight and focus will help you keep your eye on the ultimate goal.

Delay Is Not Denial

Through my work as a mentor, I have the privilege of interacting with different people from all walks of life. I have observed over time that many people genuinely acknowledge that "delay is not denial." Still, their actions and reactions are primarily discordant with the fact. Although they do believe in the well-known saying, their actions prove otherwise.

If you are experiencing a delay, or if things fail to turn out the way you expect, you ought to understand that the chances of undoing an occurrence are slim. However, you might get a different outcome if you genuinely believe that "delay is not denial." The fact that you are alive, healthy, and in the right frame of mind allows you to press the restart button and push through to make your dream a reality against all odds.

Things to Be Intentional About

Since you know that setbacks are an everyday occurrence and everyone will have their fair share of ups and downs, let us examine the 6 P's that can help you overcome them.

◊ **Prayer:** I put prayer first because prayer is the key to unlocking mysteries. I have found out that when I pray and meditate on God's Word, I find reassurance in the Scriptures. Praying and meditating on His Word helps in knowing the mystery of His will, which He outlined in Christ as a plan for the fullness of time (Ephesians 1:9-10). The next time you want to overcome a setback, pray to God; He will lessen your burden.

◊ **Planning:** I am passionate about planning. While growing up, I wrote a quote with chalk on the wall of the room I shared with my siblings: "Failing to plan is planning to fail." Many years after I got married and left my parents' house, the quote remained there. This quote is accurate to date. If you do not plan, you are planning to fail. Some people have said planning is overrated, especially since life is unpredictable. I beg to differ. My conviction is that planning is underrated.

Be intentional about planning. The truth is, engaging in planning does not guarantee that you will be free from challenges; however, it is inevitable that you will be able to measure your progress, which is vital for self-esteem. Moreover, when you experience a setback despite planning, the right step to take after hitting the roadblock will become crystal clear. This, in turn, will help you know where to restart the journey. Standing your ground amid a storm is possible with adequate planning. It gives you the ultimate sense of purpose and direction and equips you with the ability to bounce back in tough times.

◊ **Persistence**: Discouragement often creeps in during a setback. Being persistent is necessary to avoid disappearing like smoke when you experience it. Persistence is a powerful attribute that can help you overcome challenges and succeed. I can say this because I have faced setbacks many times.

I remember stories of men and women whose persistence in pursuing their dreams propelled them to succeed in what they set out to do. One such person is the famed Thomas Edison. I do not fully understand the fabric he was woven from, but I am always in awe each time I recall how he suffered a series of setbacks in his mission to create the light bulb. What type of faith could make a man try out something 10,000 times? It is called persistent faith!

If you have experienced or are currently experiencing a setback or have tried to do something you believe in many times but to no avail, is it time to raise your hands in the air and throw in the towel? Absolutely not! Problems are to be solved, and if you can be intentional about persistence, you are inching closer to overcoming your setbacks.

◊ **Play:** There have been moments when I felt like giving up on my career aspirations due to repeated failures and rejections. My efforts appeared fruitless, and I felt no point in trying anymore. However, I realized that giving up meant my chances of success would remain permanently stalled. At this point, my husband, who also served as my mentor, came to my aid. He encouraged me to persevere and reminded me of the importance of pursuing my goals, despite setbacks and challenges.

It is essential to keep playing and seek new opportunities, even when things aren't going well. It can be tempting to give up and become a spectator in your own life when faced with setbacks. However, you can only overcome obstacles and achieve your goals by continuing to play. Remember, it only takes one opportunity to turn things around and propel you to success. So, never stop playing.

◊ **Positive outlook:** Developing a positive outlook on life helps you focus on solutions rather than dwell on problems. If you retreat when there is a problem, then you reduce your chances of succeeding. When you face a problem head-on, with a can-do spirit, you increase your chances of success, and you, too, will be deemed lucky in the long run.

◊ **Perspective:** When I found myself in a college I had never dreamed of and registered for a course of study that was unpopular at the time, I struggled to see the bigger picture. There, I handled my setback as though it was the end of the road. Rather than focusing on the positive side and putting things in proper perspective, I wallowed in self-pity daily, spending a chunk of my time on trivial things. It took another setback in organic chemistry class for the scales to fall off my eyes. Today, I look back with joy and gratitude because I retraced my steps and started putting things in proper perspective.

Overcoming a setback requires that you learn to put things in proper perspective. You might discover that you need to change, alter, or even drop some of your goals, but only with the right attitude will you succeed despite the setback.

Every notable achievement demands sustained effort. The greater the action in the right direction, the greater the success. If you want astonishing success, put in extra effort and ask God to position you for divine favor. Cease resigning yourself to fate or thinking that only lucky people become successful. If you adopt an intentional disposition toward the 6 P's highlighted above, do your part, and allow God to lead. You shall succeed!

Call to Action

◊ List the lessons learned from some of the setbacks you are currently experiencing.

◊ Acknowledge your emotions and practice self-compassion when facing setbacks.

◊ Reframe the setback as an opportunity for learning and growth. Focus on solutions rather than problems.

◊ Take a break and engage in self-care activities. You can also seek support from friends, family, or mental health professionals to process emotions and gain a new perspective.

◊ Believe that delay is not denial, and take advantage of the opportunity to press the reroute button if you hit a roadblock.

◊ Be intentional about prayer and meditate on God's Word to find reassurance.

◊ Plan for the future, even though it may be unpredictable. This will help you to stay grounded and measure progress.

CHAPTER TEN

Soaring Through Limitations

"Nothing splendid has ever been achieved except by those who dared believe that something inside of them was superior to circumstance."

Bruce Barton

Since the early 1990s, my mother had dreamed of running a store in the city center. However, when the opportunity never materialized, instead of giving up, she looked within and launched her business from home. While the concept of running a business from home has become increasingly popular today, back then, my mother was one of only a few people who practiced it.

Since the early 1990s, my mother had dreamed of running a store in the city center. However, when the opportunity never materialized, she looked within and launched her business from home instead of giving up. Running a business from home has become quite popular today, but my mother was one of the few who did it back then.

As you can imagine, running a business is challenging, and doing so in a suburban area is even more demanding. With rising expenses, unpaid salaries, and a bleak economic outlook, my mother had to diversify her business ventures to keep it afloat. Against all odds, she began running a commercial pepper mill. Throughout my six years in high school, I woke up at 5 am daily to serve customers who came to grind their pepper. Although it was often out of a sense of obligation and a desire to see my mother succeed, I took on this responsibility day after day.

Despite the difficulties, my mother's determination and hard work paid off. Her business grew and thrived thanks to her willingness to adapt and try new things. Reflecting on those early mornings, I am proud of my mother's resilience and grateful for the lessons she taught me about hard work, perseverance, and dedication to one's dreams.

After years of hoping and waiting, my mother's dream of opening a store in the city center finally became a reality in the mid-2000s. She was given an incredible opportunity to use a space in the heart of the city, and her excitement knew no bounds. The space became a family project, and we spent most of our time there, helping my mother build a profitable brand.

In just a few years, my mother's business expanded, and she added two additional spaces near the first one. This allowed her to run her business precisely as she had envisioned. The journey had been difficult, but her persistence and dedication paid off, and her business thrived.

While I was working there, I had the opportunity to learn advanced strategies for converting prospects into customers, effective marketing techniques, and providing excellent customer service. The store's location was in an area with high foot traffic, so we always had to be on our toes. As a result, our daily routine was often packed, and I sometimes felt exhausted.

Soaring Through Limitations

I remember approaching my mom for a break during those challenging moments, hoping to catch my breath and recharge. However, she would look at me and smile. Looking back, I realize that my mother was not just a businesswoman but also a mentor who understood the value of hard work and perseverance.

My mother helped me develop skills that have served me well personally and professionally by pushing me beyond my limits. Her unwavering belief in my potential gave me the confidence to tackle challenging tasks and persevere through difficult times.

After spending considerable time working alongside my mother in her business, the time finally came for me to start a new chapter by getting married and pursuing my dreams. As I left to start my new journey, my mother continued to run her business with the same passion and dedication that had made it a success.

For several years, her business continued to thrive and grow, and it seemed like nothing could stop her. However, one day, I received a call from her with heartbreaking news. Two of her spaces had been marked for demolition due to a road expansion project in the city.

It was a devastating blow, and my mother was understandably upset. The thought of losing a significant portion of her business was overwhelming, and she struggled to accept it.

"Is there any plan in place by the government?" I asked.

Of course, you can guess what her response was. There was no real plan put in place by the government to assist those affected. My heart sank as I began to think about my mom's sacrifices to grow profitable brands. The demolition was a major disruption for my mom and the entire family, leaving us with one question: "What next?"

Reinventing After a Major Disruption

Following the demolition of two of her spaces due to the city's road expansion project, my mother was left with deciding her next move. It wasn't easy, but after recovering and reassessing her situation, she pivoted to a new industry. I was initially skeptical about her chances of success in this new field, but my mom's determination and grit proved me wrong.

I was impressed by her level of commitment and how she reinvented herself. She had a well-thought-out plan, which showed her clear intentions and determination to succeed, even when the odds were not in her favor. Her plan involved extensive market research and analysis, identifying potential niches, and developing a comprehensive business strategy.

After pivoting her business, my mom remained unwavering in her pursuit of success. She worked tirelessly, dedicating herself to her duties and showing up every day, rain or shine. Her resilience and determination were unmatched, and she refused to let any obstacle deter her from achieving her goals. Her work ethic was a testament to her character and left a lasting impression on everyone who knew her. Despite adversity, disruptions, and challenges, my mom remained steadfast and committed to her craft until her passing.

What disruption have you suffered or are you currently experiencing? Know that no matter the magnitude of the disruption, you always have the choice of reinventing yourself. Experiencing storms, problems, or challenges is a normal part of life. And when push comes to shove, always remember that you can choose to reinvent yourself after a major disruption and go on to succeed in life against all odds.

Receiving the Call That Made a Difference

One of the primary goals I set each year is to host the Power Woman Experience (PWE), an annual story-sharing event for business and professional women worldwide to learn, connect, collaborate, and network with one another.

As the pandemic continued to worsen, the possibility of hosting an in-person gathering for the 2020 edition of the event became increasingly uncertain. Faced with this daunting challenge, I contemplated canceling the entire event. It was the logical decision, given the circumstances. However, my daughter's unwavering enthusiasm and passion for the event inspired me to reconsider. Despite the uncertainty of the situation, she remained focused on finding a way to make it happen.

A short while later, I received a call from one of my Kingdom sisters who wanted to know how far I had gone with the plans for the event. I repeated the same reasons and excuses I offered my daughter, and she allowed me to complete my supposed justification.

"Are you done?" she asked.

"Yes, I am done," I responded.

"We are planning PWE 2020 against all odds! This is an opportunity to impact on a broader scale, and you should go for it," she stated. Her words ran deep!

The call from my Kingdom sister turned out to be a turning point in my perspective on the pandemic. Initially, I was still determining if I could deliver a successful virtual event, but my daughter's encouragement and support made me reconsider. I began to see it as an opportunity rather than a setback. It was like a light switch went on in my brain, and I realized that there was still a way to move forward with the event despite the pandemic.

Additionally, I prayed about my decision to host the event virtually and commit it to God's hands. That was how we pivoted PWE from an in-person to an online event in 2020. It was a challenging process, but the experience of putting it together was rewarding, and the event turned out to be the most impactful one I had ever hosted at the time. We had participants from all over the world, and the feedback was overwhelmingly positive.

Circumventing Limitations

Following the success of the 2020 edition of the Power Woman Experience event, I felt inspired to continue interviewing individuals who overcame significant obstacles to achieve success, both to motivate myself and others.

During this period, a friend and fellow entrepreneur introduced me to Mrs. Ayodeji Megbope, the CEO of No Leftovers, a thriving catering business. What amazed me about her story was that she began her brand with only ₦1,000, equivalent to just $3 at the time. Despite facing limitations that could have hindered her success, Mrs. Megbope refused to be held back and soared to greater heights. I have decided to share an abridged version of my interview with her.

The Interview

Q: Please introduce yourself.

A: My name is Ayodeji Megbope. I have been married for 27 years, and my husband and I are blessed with two amazing children. I run a catering business in Lagos, Nigeria, and I have been doing this for 13 years. I started with a capital of ₦1,000 and began with moimoi4, like practically hawking moimoi. Today, it has grown and is still growing. I am grateful to God for the steps He has given us the grace to take, for the favor of being able to rise from the position of hopelessness to where I have found myself today, and indeed for all the people who have been part of my journey.

Q: What were you doing before you started No Leftovers as a business?

A: Growing up was full of twists and turns for me. But just before starting No Leftovers, I had worked there for 9 years, so I have 20 years of work experience. I worked as a secretary for all those 20 years. Apart from being a secretary, I did business here and there. However, my primary work was being a secretary, and my only place of work was at Corona School, Ikoyi. As I said, I worked for 9 years, and my children were privileged to have attended that school.

In the 9th year of working at Corona School Ikoyi, I became exhausted and asked myself,

"Is that all there is to be?..."

Something else that unsettled my feelings then was because I was going to clock 40. Although turning 40 is supposed to be a significant landmark in life — the age many people often celebrate — I did not look forward to any celebration in my case. At the time, I suddenly looked at my life and felt there was nothing to write home about. I began to feel like I could do something different, so I asked God what to do.

My children were always excited to listen to the stories of some people and how their lives had turned around for the better, and I began to long for the same story to be told about me. How could I change the narratives so far? I realized that if I did not want to continue to undergo what I had been experiencing all my life, I needed to do something differently. That informed my decision to resign from Corona School Ikoyi as a secretary.

I did not have a lot of qualifications at that time. All I had was a diploma in secretarial administration that I obtained, but it made me feel scared. I needed to be more skilled to venture into other areas. Yet, I told myself that something had to happen because I had come across people who did not even go to school and had made meaning out of their lives. Therefore, I dared to step out.

Q: What was the plan? What gave you the confidence to resign? What were you looking forward to doing after your resignation?

A: These are exciting questions. I believed this because I had been hearing success stories from people who didn't have elaborate qualifications but could still create meaningful lives through their skills and abilities. Their experiences inspired me to seek more purpose in my own life. In all honesty, I did not have a specific plan. I just knew that I could not step out without thinking of something, so I looked at my immediate environment at the time and asked myself a critical question:

"What would I love to do?"

It was tough because my experiences of failure had hit me in a way, although I was oblivious to it. Since I had worked in a structured environment all my life, I never thought about it. In truth, I enjoyed working in a school environment for all of those years, even though I did not have a degree in education. Since I am a mother, I decided to open a daycare center. That was my initial plan.

Soaring Through Limitations

Q: How did you move from wanting a daycare center to starting a business with ₦1,000 while cooking and selling moimoi?

A: When I resigned, I attended training to equip myself to set up a daycare business. Upon the completion of that training, I experienced a tremendous sense of dissatisfaction.

> I said, "I have only lived this life for 40 years. Is this what I want to do now? Do I know what this business entails?"

I was sincere with myself, and I said No! I truly loved caring for children, but I discovered that owning a daycare center required more than loving children. So, once again, I went back to my husband to tell him what I felt,

> and he said, "Look, I believe in you. Keep pushing, praying, believing in God, and doing what you know is best."

Even though I did not establish a daycare center, the knowledge I gained during the training was well-spent. What I eventually did while waiting was to offer my services to the parents who requested a home tutor, and I was blessed to have four children. At the time, I taught the children for one hour, three days a week, and they came from two families. Both families had two children each, allowing me to earn an income while waiting for what I wanted to do.

Now, talking about how I started the business of moimoi. The children I was teaching were the sons and daughters of the elite, and they frequently traveled during the summer break. As a result, it led to a loss of income during the holiday. Then, one fateful day, I told my husband there was no food in the house, and he said, "I trust you. All I have is this."

When he said that, I thought he had so much money because his body language revealed self-confidence. I thought, "Wow, this guy had some money, but he did not tell me anything about it!" Only for my husband to hand over ₦1,000 to me. I was tempted to let him know he was in denial, but somehow I held my peace.

I can never forget that day because it reminds me of what my mother used to tell me. She would say, "When you are married, you must always have some charms. The charms are like an invisible bottle of water you put in your mouth, but refrain from swallowing until your anger abates. The charms came in handy that day as I kept mute, collected the ₦1,000, and headed to the market to buy the ingredients for making moimoi.

Later on in the evening, my sister-in-law visited us. She tasted the moimoi, liked it, and asked me to make it for her. I told her I would prepare it if she could give me ₦1,000. She did. I made the moimoi for her the next day and shared the leftovers with my neighbor. Shortly after I gave it to my neighbor, she came knocking and said,

> "Oh my goodness! The moimoi is so nice! Can you make it for me?"

> "Oh yes! If you give me ₦1,000, I will make it for you," I responded.

My sister-in-law also gave it to her friend, who found it delicious. My sister-in-law told her friend the amount it would cost her if she wanted me to make it for her.

That was how I started selling moimoi as everybody asked me the same question:

Soaring Through Limitations

"Can you please make moimoi for me?"

So gradually, I witnessed ₦1,000 evolving into ₦5,000 and then into ₦10,000. Thirteen years down the line, here we are.

Q: I am curious why you did not ask people for ₦2,000 or ₦3,000. Were you not thinking of making it a business, then?

A: I was clueless, and it did not occur to me that it would ever become a business; I had never heard of it.

Q: At what point did you decide to take the selling of moimoi seriously?

A: It began when I saw how ₦1,000 increased to ₦5,000, and I started keeping records. Things were quite challenging for the family, such that we ended up living on the proceeds from the sales of moimoi. Our daughter was my cashier then, and at the end of each day, no matter how tough, I told her to set aside ₦100. It was beautiful to watch the money grow.

Q: How were you able to go back to your former place of work, where you were a secretary, to sell moimoi? Did you decide to do what you needed without thinking about what people would say?

A: I had lived all 40 years of my life considering what people would say. When I began to see the proceeds from the sales of moimoi, my perspective on life changed, and I began to appreciate myself.

I returned to Corona School Ikoyi because sales began to dwindle after selling to family, friends, and church members for a while. When I thought about where to go to increase sales, the school I had worked at was the only place that came to mind since I knew I could sell to many people who already knew me then.

Q: What are the top three challenges in your business so far, and how were you able to solve them?

A: The first thing I needed to deal with was myself. I know everyone faces challenges, but being able to convince myself that I was strong and good enough and that I could set up the business was very taxing. Secondly, I have had different challenges in my relationships.

I have discovered that being in touch eliminates many hurdles, especially in a good association or a circle of people at the right time. I could never have come this far without the gift of relationships.

My business could only have reached this milestone with the likes of Goldman Sachs and Enterprise for Development Center, among others. These are institutions, but people run them. Without them, especially my testimony at the White House during Barack Obama's administration, I would not have gone this far.

Some people have asked me,

> "Ayo, you speak about your journey to the White House. Can you please share how I can connect myself with top people?"

Those who would help you reach your next level are never clad in conspicuous "help garments." If you live with the mindset of appreciating everybody that comes your way, you can take advantage of opportunities when they appear.

The last challenge is fear. Sometimes I woke up in the morning and thought about the loan I had taken due to having planned, done feasibility studies, and projected that this job was coming, yet COVID-19 suddenly hit the world.

How do I handle it? Should I bury my head under my duvet and refuse to come out? Should I shut down? No! I went to the organization I borrowed from and asked, "Can I discuss it with you?" I found out that they can only harass you when you hide. But you will make headway when you are proactive and do not allow fear to limit you.

I have had situations where they told me that I was an honorable woman, that they could give me more time to pay off the loan, or even write it off. I have seen amazing things happen. Some wrote off my debt, while others told me I must pay. Then I replied to them that I would surely pay the loan. But here I am today. Look at my business. I intended to be honest and eliminate fear. Fear can be confusing, crippling, and tormenting, making it difficult to think clearly and find a way out of a situation.

Q: Can you please tell the audience about the application process of Goldman Sachs and how you got selected?

A: Okay, let me tell you something. When I gave my life to Christ, I discovered that the word works. I started searching the Scriptures for what word I could hold on to that showed a similitude to where I wanted to be. What is in Isaiah 60 was what I found. And for over 30 years, I have been confessing Isaiah 60 almost daily.

What you desire is what you attract. You will never attract what you despise. It is unlikely that you will attract the success that person has achieved. So peradventure, you go through somebody's Instagram page and see that the person is doing so well, and your heart is full of bitterness, hatred, and anger; you are already despising that person. When I learned that, I began to yearn to celebrate others and desire to return to school.

Later on, I saw on the pages of a newspaper that Goldman Sachs Group was coming to invest in women. At first, I was not qualified because they were doing it in conjunction with the Enterprise for Development Center, which is under Lagos Business School. But I thank God for cheerleaders, especially my husband.

I approached my husband and said,

"See this newspaper advert, but I do not think I am qualified."

"Ayo, stop saying that. If you try and you are not selected, you will know you have at least tried," he told me.

Q: What are your top three lessons, and what were your reactions when you started getting invitations from global platforms?

A: Success is not the exclusive right of anybody; you can succeed if you attempt to. The second lesson is that you can be anything you want to be. Speak about it, continue to work toward it, and you will become it. The third lesson is always to appreciate the power of prayers. How did I feel when I got such invitations? Well, the feeling has changed now. My initial feeling the first time I was invited to the United States was unbelief — I was blown away! Sooner or later, you will be like those you associate yourself with. It started with a lot of excitement and gratitude to God. But as I continued to follow Him, it occurred to me that it was not about me. My life has come to a point where I know that every platform is for an assignment.

Call to Action

◊ Take the time to heal when facing a major disruption, and then reinvent yourself by taking the next action.

◊ Recognize the opportunities that may present themselves in challenges, and be open to pivoting or adapting to new circumstances in times of crisis.

◊ Consider looking for alternatives whenever you have run out of options rather than giving up.

◊ Draw inspiration from people who have defied great odds to achieve success in life.

◊ Identify what you love to do and take steps to make it a reality. Be honest with yourself about your capabilities and interests.

◊ Commit your plans to God's hands. Modify them when necessary, and continue pushing, praying, and believing in yourself and God.

Conclusion

Wow! You made it till the end - you deserve a pat on the back. One of my goals is to let you know you were born with the potential for greatness, regardless of any limitations or excuses you may have. This potential exists in people of all genders, ages, locations, religious affiliations, and educational and socioeconomic backgrounds. It is a divine gift from God, and it is up to each person to cultivate and nurture it.

It is crucial to rise above challenges and limitations, push through adversity, and find ways to overcome obstacles. By realizing their potential, individuals can achieve extraordinary things and fulfill their purpose in life. Moreover, they can inspire and empower those around them to do the same.

You have within you the power to create positive change in your life and the world. With determination, hard work, and a willingness to take risks, you can blaze a trail and achieve your dreams. Remember, you are not alone in your journey; some people believe in you and count on you to fulfill your destiny. So go forth, spread your wings, and soar to new heights against all odds!

How Do You "See" the Glass?

Did the COVID-19 pandemic leave you feeling defeated and hopeless? Did it seem like all your plans were shattered, leaving you with no control over your future? I know that feeling all too well. Despite the advice I often give others about seeing the positive side of things, it was challenging to do the same when faced with the pandemic.

However, I soon realized I needed to take my advice and change my perspective. Instead of seeing the glass as half empty, I needed to see it as half full. This shift in mindset was crucial to my ability to adapt and continue making an impact despite the setbacks.

Having people around me who offered encouragement and support also made a huge difference. It reminded me of the power of community and the importance of leaning on others during difficult times.

So, how do you see the glass? Do you focus on what you've lost or what you still have? It's easy to feel defeated, but with a positive mindset and a supportive community, you can overcome any challenge and become stronger on the other side.

Have You Done Your Part?

One top lesson learned from the pandemic is that it's essential to receive counsel from people who genuinely care about our well-being. However, more is needed to receive advice; we need to take responsibility for our actions and try to implement the guidance we receive.

While some situations might be beyond our control, we still have the power to control our reactions and actions. It's vital to understand that success is not achieved by sitting idle or giving up but by taking action toward achieving our goals.

In challenging situations, thinking of ways to solve the problem is crucial rather than giving up. Trying to contribute opens up opportunities for God to show up and work things out in our favor. For example, PWE 2020 looked only possible once stakeholders came together and went above and beyond the call of duty to make it happen.

Asking for Help

Another top takeaway from 2020 is remembering to ask for help. On a personal note, I saw beauty in asking for help because most of the things we need are within close range. However, once we ask, we may be able to access many of the resources we need to move to the next level.

Besides, God put people — old and young — in our lives for a purpose. Therefore, the onus is on us to build cordial relationships with others to have a solid support system we can ask to help us when we truly need it. When was the last time you asked for help? Always remember that asking is the beginning of receiving. If you fail to ask, you will hardly receive.

One of my favorite Bible verses is Proverbs 15:22: "Plans fail for lack of counsel, but with many advisers they succeed." I would have lost a great opportunity had I decided to cancel PWE 2020. Thankfully, I have people around me who want the best for me, and they are always looking for ways to help me serve my audience in a higher capacity. Not only did hosting the event assist me in developing new skills, but it also counted toward helping me fulfill my purpose. I am in awe each time I read the feedback from attendees and the multiple returns those who keyed in are getting from their investments.

Moving Forward Against All Odds

To move forward against all odds, defining your objectives and recognizing the barriers in your path is crucial. From there, it is vital to create a detailed plan of action that allows you to surmount or sidestep these challenges. Your plan should adhere to the principles of being specific, measurable, achievable, relevant, and time-bound (SMART), leaving no room for uncertainty or ambiguity.

In addition to a solid plan of action, a positive attitude, a strong sense of purpose and determination, and self-belief are crucial to moving forward against all odds. I have personally overcome many obstacles in life by cultivating a responsible attitude. While writing this book, I encountered numerous roadblocks that delayed the progress. However, I resolved to keep pushing forward, no matter what, and as a result, my dream has become a reality today. This same principle has helped countless others overcome seemingly insurmountable obstacles and achieve great success in life.

Another key to moving forward against all odds is to surround yourself with supportive and visionary individuals is crucial to overcoming obstacles and achieving success.

These individuals may be close friends, family members, or mentors who can offer guidance and encouragement during challenging times. However, to gain their support, your vision must be compelling, and your dedication to it must be evident. They want to see that you are willing to persevere and overcome obstacles rather than giving up at the first sign of difficulty. It is also essential to remain flexible and adaptable, willing to try new approaches to problem-solving as circumstances change.

Finally, be unrelenting in your effort. Success is rarely achieved easily, and it often requires hard work, dedication, and a willingness to push through, even when it seems like nothing is going your way. It is important to remember that setbacks and failures are a natural process. When you encounter challenges, do not give up. Instead, use the setbacks as an opportunity to learn, adjust your approach, and keep pushing forward.

Being persistent also means staying focused on your goals, even when you face distractions or temptations. It requires a deep sense of commitment and the ability to keep the course, even when others around you may be giving up. It also requires the willingness to keep trying new approaches, even when you have failed in the past.

So, to succeed in life against all odds, you must be persistent. You must be willing to work hard, stay focused on your goals, and keep trying new approaches until you find what works. Success may take time, but with persistence and determination, you can achieve it.

So, to sum up, if you want to achieve success in life against all odds, you must be persistent. You must be willing to work hard, stay focused on your goals, and keep trying new approaches until you find what works. Success may take time, but with persistence and determination, you can achieve it.

Bibliography

"Life is progress and not a station." Emerson, Ralph Waldo. Essays by Ralph Waldo Emerson. DigiCat, 2022.

"Nothing can resist the human will that will stake even its existence on its stated purpose." Barnum, P. T., et al. SELF-MASTERY: 30 Best Books to Guide You to Your Goals: The Collected Wisdom From the Greatest Books on Becoming Wealthy and Successful. e-artnow, 2019.

"The greater clarity you have about who you are and what you want, the more you will achieve and the faster you will achieve it in every area of your life." Tracy, Brian. Goals!: How to Get Everything You Want-Faster Than You Ever Thought Possible. ReadHowYouWant.com, 2008.

"If you want to accomplish a dream, you will be able to do so when you can see it. You must define it before you can pursue it. Most people do not do that. Their dreams remain a dream — something fuzzy and unspecific. As a result, they never achieve it." Maxwell, John C. Put Your Dream to the Test: 10 Questions That Will Help You See It and Seize It. Thomas Nelson Inc, 2011.

"The heights that great men reached and kept were not attained by sudden flight, but they, while their companions slept, were toiling upward in the night." College, Cheltenham. The Cheltonian. 1867.

"Proper Prior Planning Prevents Poor Performance." Tracy, Brian. Goals!: How to Get Everything You Want - Faster Than You Ever Thought Possible. ReadHowYouWant.com, 2008.

"For those who exalt themselves will be humbled, and those who humble themselves will be exalted." Matthew

23:12. Version, New International. Holy Bible: N.I.V. New International Version. New International Version, 2011.

"Practice is not the thing you do once you are good. It is the thing you do that makes you good." Gladwell, Malcolm. Outliers: The Story of Success. Penguin UK, 2008.

"The 10,000-Hour Rule." Gladwell, Malcolm. Outliers: The Story of Success. Penguin UK, 2008.

"We will either find a way or make one." We Will Either Find a Way or Make One: 6 X9 120 Pages Journal. 2020.

"The will to win, the desire to succeed, the urge to reach your full potential; these are the keys that will unlock the door to personal excellence." Arbitrament, Si. Confucius Notebook: The Will to Win the Desire to Succeed the Urge to Reach Your Full Potential These Are the Keys That Will Unlock the Door to Personal Excellence. 2019.

"Ask and it will be given to you; seek and you will find; knock and the door will be opened to you." Matthew 7:7. Version, New International. Holy Bible: N.I.V. New International Version. New International Version, 2011.

"Potential is a priceless treasure, like gold. All of us have gold hidden within, but we have to dig to get it out." Meyer, Joyce. A Leader in the Making: Essentials to Being a Leader After God's Own Heart. Hachette UK, 2008.

"Your success in today's globalized world requires an ability to adapt to a variety of cultural situations." Livermore, David. The Cultural Intelligence Difference: Master the One Skill You Can't Do Without in Today's Global Economy. AMACOM, 2011.

"Definition of Culture." Merriam-Webster Dictionary, 24 Jan. 2023, www.merriam-webster.com/diction-

Bibliography

ary/culture#:~:text=cul%C2%B7%E2%80%8Bture%20%CB%88k%C9%99l%2Dch%C9%99r,popular%20culture.

"is the capability to function effectively across a variety of cultural contexts, such as ethnic, generational, and organizational cultures." Livermore, David. The Cultural Intelligence Difference: Master the One Skill You Can't Do Without in Today's Global Economy. AMACOM, 2011.

"Setbacks are inevitable; misery is a choice." Covey, Stephen R. The 8th Habit: From Effectiveness to Greatness. Simon and Schuster, 2013.

Khemchandani, Madhsudhan. "Canva User and Company Stats (2023)." MKs Guide, 22 Mar. 2023, www.mksguide.com/canva-user-stats.

"a rational being can turn each setback into raw material and use it to achieve its goal." Aurelius, Marcus. Meditations. Signature Classics, 2022.

"Nothing splendid has ever been achieved except by those who dared believe that something inside of them was superior to circumstance." Wattles, Wallace D., et al. A Road to Prosperity - Ultimate Collection. e-artnow, 2022.

"Plans fail for lack of counsel, but with many advisers they succeed." Proverbs 15:22. Version, New International. Holy Bible: N.I.V. New International Version. New International Version, 2011.

Glossary

1. akara: A Nigerian food made by deep frying beans, pepper and onion paste.

2. Sokoto: A state located in northwestern Nigeria.

3. sokoto: A pair of trousers.

4. moimoi: Nigerian savory steamed pudding made from ground black-eyed peas, pepper, onions, etc.

About Seun Akinlotan

Seun Akinlotan is a multifaceted professional who has made her mark in various fields. She is an Environmental Scientist, Adjunct Instructor, Life Coach, Trainer, Speaker, Entrepreneur and Author.

Growing up in the suburbs of Rock City, Ogun State, Nigeria, Seun was inspired by her mother's extraordinary achievements and aspired to make a lasting impact on the lives of women worldwide. With this vision in mind, she founded the Seun Akinlotan Network (SAN), a revolutionary mentorship platform that helps women maximize their potential and live their best lives. She is also the convener of the Power Woman Experience (thepowerwomanexperience.com), an annual event where women gather to share their inspiring stories of overcoming challenges and achieving success in their careers or businesses.

As a teacher and mentor, Seun has a gift for inspiring and motivating those around her. Her John Maxwell certification as a coach, speaker, and trainer makes her a highly sought-after speaker on leadership, personal development, and financial independence.

In her personal life, Seun is happily married with two adorable children. She enjoys cooking, biking, or attending a class when not engaged in her work. To learn more about her and her work, visit her website at seunakinlotan.com.

www.ingramcontent.com/pod-product-compliance
Lightning Source LLC
Chambersburg PA
CBHW070600010526
44118CB00012B/1399